SLEEPING NAKED AFTER 40

A Woman's Inspirational, Motivational, and Educational Guide
to Extreme Self-Care and Love

THIS BOOK BELONGS TO:
_____

DATE:
_____

(You will want to record and remember this date—the day you decided to love yourself enough to change your body and your life for the better.)

Loving Gratitude

An extreme thank you to my three beautiful children, Randy, Mike, and Katie, who are my inspiration and joy, and to whom I am beyond grateful for the lessons they have taught me about myself, love, and the world.

They inspire me, push me, and love me into being my best, every day, in every way, in everything I do. I am in awe of the beautiful, productive, energetic, giving adults they have become.

Special thanks to Katie O. for her spunky attitude and fire that trigger intense conversation, debate and creativity. It is because of her talented writing skills, her ability to see things as they are, and her quick fingers on the delete button that you are not reading five hundred pages.

This community of amazing people surrounds me with LOVE and provides incentive to me to do more and be more everyday!

Contents

TOPIC
Welcome to Sleeping Naked After 40
(Moving) Forward
Lesson Breakdown
The Commitment
The Inspiration: Strength Beyond Muscles

Lessons

Lesson	Topic	Your Body (Nutrition Transition)	Your Head (SMACK)	YUM (Naked Recipes)	Your Heart
1	The Choice	Careful Choices	You Choose	Strawberry Almond Dressing	Get off the Bench
2	The Morning Attitude	Your First Meal of the Day	It's All In Your Attitude	Oatmeal Bars	Breakfast Menu Experiment
3	Cheers to Sleeping Naked	Drink It	Affirm It	Hot Cinnamon Ginger Water	Make it/ Tape it
4	Green Cleans and Clean Leans	Eat more Greens	Go Green	Dressing the Greens	Let it Go, Baby
5	Lose the Fake Stuff and Get Real	Think Outside the Box	Ditch and Switch	PB & J, the Naked Way	Kitchen Cabinet Pitch

Lesson	Topic	Your Body (Nutrition Transition)	Your Head (SMACK)	YUM (Naked Recipes)	Your Heart
6	Falling in Love... with yourself	Body Kindness	Xtreme to Xtraordinary	Meat "Less" Loaf	How I Love Thee
7	Are We There Yet?	Fat Chance	Pant Chants — Diet Speak	Avocado/Blueberry Shake	Retrain your brain
8	Become less interested in why you can't	Naked Fuel	Replace Disappointment with an Appointment	Chocolate Energy Bars	Grow Yourself
9	This and Thats	Your Power Prescription	On and On	Yum-azing Fun Pop	Lose the Excuse
10	What's on Your Plate?	Naked Eating	Get Down to It	Dreamy Naked Chocolate	The Chocolate Challenge/ The Body Challenge
11	You Deserve It	Treat Yourself Well	Make it up to Yourself	Scones	What's on the menu?
12	Sleeping Naked	Don't Be a Bag lady	Use your Pretty Head	Power Pancakes	Your Dream Book

ADDENDUM
Big Bonus
YOU Are Amazing
Resource Guide: "Think Outside the Box" BOX with Sleeping Naked Tools
Thank You Again
Supplemental Experience Experiment Workbook Section

Just for you, my fabulous over 40 women,
love enlarged the font size of my book.
Need I say more?

Welcome to Sleeping Naked

This book was written over the four-year period of my personal journey of self-discovery, healing, and transformation. My own struggles and similar problems conveyed to me by clients and friends prompted me to take the lead and find solutions that would benefit a society of women with shared concerns. Women plagued by out-of-control eating, "disordered" relationships with food, feeling overwhelmed, and decreased self-esteem found themselves exhibiting their troubles through excess body weight.

I wanted answers, and I needed support; yet only when I was ready and willing to listen, were they delivered. Neither the answers nor the support arrived all at once, but instead in bite-sized, digestible pieces from a staggering collection of expected and unexpected sources – a passing stranger, a response to a prayer, meditation, research and classes. My random thoughts were written on scraps of paper and collected in a box, until my box was full and the only option was to put it all together in this book.

Back in the day, (I just love that I can say that now as one of the perks of being half way to fulfillment, i.e.: middle-aged) in grammar school, I was a quiet, speechless, little, good girl with no voice of her own. Hell, there was no one listening, or so I thought. I was taught to be quiet – a big surprise, I know, to those of you who know me now. I went to Catholic school where you didn't speak unless spoken to, and as one of five children, raised by extremely young and busy parents, at home there wasn't much time for individual expression or listening. You got the stare down, and you shut up. It was that simple. I was totally convinced that I didn't have much to say that was important, and even if I did, it wasn't important enough for an audience. These limiting beliefs stopped me from writing because I never seemed able to put into words what I really felt. This was a considerable factor in my "disordered" eating, as I used food to stuff down whatever I couldn't say. I didn't realize it then, but in hindsight, I see that my pen and ink drawings, colorful painted canvases, vintage sewn fashion designs, and molded clay creations were silent expressions of my untold story.

As I got older and developed the nerve to write, I always had someone correcting me, either when I asked for the support and even when I didn't. Not that long ago, when I wrote the personal essay (based on my experience) about how the decision to participate in a body-building competition transformed my life, a partner I was working with at the time, decided (this was one of the unsolicited opinions) to correct my story. He told me it would read better if I deleted a few points and didn't tell the whole thing. That incident shook me to my core and was the turning point for publishing this book when I realized, I did have something important to say and to share.

Okay, so now I am worse than a transformed smoker, and as a transformed non verbal or written communicator, I'm making up for lost time or rather words - I am a talk-a-holic, passionate about my message and getting the word out about being healthy and sexy at every age. I am an author with several books, workbooks and Cooklets © in print and more in the pipeline.

When I gave up on perfectionism, let go of the fear of judgment and criticism and just let my voice and message rip, I began to rock the real deal and help others change their lives for the better. Sleeping Naked After 40 is real and naked, with perhaps some lovingly missed typos, grammatical mishaps or overlooks (which I am sure will make my mom cringe as those are some of her pet peeves). I apologize ahead of time, but what really matters is that you take these ideas and suggestions and get them working for you in your own life. Focus on the things that relate to you and your story and pursue your own path to Nakedness.

I am super grateful for the opportunity to share these inspirations and ideas with you and motivate you to grow, learn, and overcome your own struggles with food, nourishment, self confidence, and self love.

UGH! UNCOMFORTABLE FEELINGS SUCK (and suck the life out of you).

It's very uncomfortable feeling uncomfortable in your own skin. You are living in this body everyday, so being uncomfortable at your core is far from rocking a big party. I know this from experience.

I am Rosie Battista and I sleep naked. This wasn't always the case. I was one very uncomfortable girl. I struggled most of my life with fluctuating weight, self esteem and body image. I could move the scale up 20 and down 20 within weeks through starving and binging, and I did it well. So well that no one ever knew. I struggled and suffered alone, with no awareness that I had the option to change. Maintaining an obsessive focus on trying to lose the 20 pounds I gained kept me diverted and so occupied I didn't have time to look at the real issues that needed to change in my life.

Over-weight is not just about the additional, uncomfortable pounds that we carry on our bodies and that show up as the dreaded number on the scale. Over-weight is what shows up when we are not nourishing or caring for ourselves. Simply put, when you eat fake, processed, white, refined, chemically-infused substances (they call it "fast" food, but I call it crap food), it will show up on your body- mainly in your middle and then it creeps all over the place. When you care and nourish yourself with pure and naked food, the body of your dreams shows up. You may not be ready to embrace this fully yet but here is my simplest advice on food - there is no white stuff after 40! Eliminating processed flours and sugars is a great starting place to clean up your food act.

One day I did the math. Holy crap! The sum of the weight I'd lost, gained, re-lost, regained, etc., etc. was 600 pounds. What's your equation look like? Multiply your number of years dieting times number of pounds you lost and found again. Looking at the number is a jolt, slam, bang, smack in the head. Your eye opener. Maybe it's what you need as your reality check to start you on the road to getting real.

Back in the day, I bought into the diet myth; I ate for the sole purpose of weight loss, or rather I deprived myself for weight loss. I was grabbing every restricted and low carb, low calorie and fake food product that claimed to produce those results. If it came in a box with a calorie count and claim, that was my dinner. Got any use for a 7' high pillar of diet books? I got 'em and can save you the trouble of reading them; they didn't make a long-term difference for me unless you consider the exercise I get toting them around. Yeah they all worked while I was on them, but as soon as I got "there" (reached my goal weight), I put the pounds right back on. It got so confusing, and even more frustrating. I mean how on earth was I supposed to figure out what to do? What worked forever, rather than just for the moment? Sound familiar?

A 10-year-old girl, my beautiful little daughter put it all into proper perspective when she made it very clear what I was doing to myself and, in the process, teaching her. One day she stepped on the scale at that ripe young age and said "Mom, I'm fat". For me that was a knock in the head, my wake up call, and shock enough to set my wheels for change in motion.

And so, I started on this path to real health, self care and self love. And it all started with food. I have tons of education and certifications in nutrition that you can check out in the back of this book but the reason that I can really help you is that I get it. I understand you, where you are coming from and how challenging the road to self care can be. I also understand that even though it seems challenging, it is do-able. You can do it!

That 40th birthday candle is not an indisputable recipe for a muffin top, low energy, low libido, and feeling fat and frumpy (though the birthday cake may be!). It is precisely because you are over forty that you should look and feel rockin' hot, healthy and sexy. Because now you are not only beautiful, you are smart and experienced, too. You can have it all for the first time in your life. Take advantage of the best years of your life; accept the beautiful, magnificent person that you are. I will teach you to fall in love – with the real you, starting with the food you eat and the body you build by eating the right foods.

I'm not handing you your good health o

n a silver platter, mind you, you've got some work to do and some changes to make. But I'll lead the way to show you how, and give you a chance to customize the program to suit your personal taste. Together we'll prove that change is to be embraced, not feared, and you'll be rewarded by feeling and looking fabulous. You are on your way to becoming the best person you can be, physically, emotionally and spiritually. Why, may I ask, would you want it any other way?

So set those creaky, old, lethargic, bones in action first by turning a few pages. This guide to extreme self care and love is just what you need to get the ball rolling and get you rockin'. There is beauty and discovery at every age and every stage. You are a gift to this world and the only way that you can present your best stuff is for you to become your best self. Let's begin the process of falling in love.

I'll start by sharing 3 secrets to self love. They are easy to remember and they make all the difference in every aspect of your life. I would write them down and tape them to the refrigerator door. But hey, that's me. If you came over for tea, you'd see that I have quotations, inspirational, motivational, mantras and affirmations everywhere just in case my self esteem lags a bit and I need to regain focus to be all that I am and all that I will continue to grow to become. Feel free to copy my tactic and do the same for yourself. Subliminally I believe it has power in switching the way you think and see things. The glass is never half empty in this world anymore, and I've got a saying on my fridge that reminds me of that.

The secrets revealed (drum roll, please):

1. Lose the fake stuff and get real (and get your body in the game)
2. Become less interested in why you can't (and get your head in the game)
3. Fall in love with the idea of being and eating better (and get your heart in the game)

These 3 secrets are the basis for everything I do starting with my food. They can be applied to this game of weight loss and physical body image and to all aspects of your life; exercise, career, relationships, family.

One discovery from having so many diet/self help books is that I would buy the books, start "the program" and more often than not, never finish. I'd move off and onto the next newest and best plan that came out. Every one of these diet/nutrition books is chock full of so much, sometimes contradictory information that it could make your head spin. Every author is adamant that his or her way is the best way. Follow this, follow that, count this, don't count that, eat carbs, don't eat carbs, be a vegan, be a vegetarian, go raw, countless restrictions, and…yikes! Okay, so YES, they do work when you are on them. But when you are off them, what do you do? Even if one way made complete sense to you, and even if you were able to follow it for a while, it wouldn't last. Even if you have amazing information in front of you, how do you actually implement all that they ask of you and do it consistently?

If you want this time to be different, you need to be different in your approach. You need to be all in. What I mean by that is that you need to make the decision to commit and get your heart and head in the game. So ladies, start by making a plan of action for reading and experiencing Sleeping Naked After 40.

Sleeping Naked After 40 (SNAF) is divided into 12 lessons. I did that purposely because it fits nicely into a result-oriented time frame. 12 months means a year of change, 12 weeks is just about the amount of time needed to see changes develop into new habits. These 12 lessons can be approached in many different ways and only you can decide the best way for you. You are in charge and must choose the way that will work for you.

Don't be too aggressive in your decision. I mean, you know how on the first of the new year, everyone is at the gym, (people you haven't seen since last January 2nd) committing once again to the newest workout every day, 2 hours a day. Now we also know that that momentum lasts about a couple of weeks before burn out kicks in followed by the towel thrown in and the gym membership thrown out.. Give yourself permission to choose a pace that feels right to you and works for your life. Be patient. One cookie did not make you fat, and one week of extreme self care is not going to fix all the issues. As little as one week of consistent extreme self care will, however, make you feel better.

Remember: This is all about you. You are participating in an experience of extreme self care and love. It is your choice, and all about your body. There is no right way—there is only your way. Remember that this book is your "work" book and you are a "work" in progress. You can always go back and redo, revisit, revamp and renew any challenges or lessons as needed. I even included an addendum in the back with additional space in so you can redo the exercise experiences.

You have a chance to check off the option that works for you and commit to completing it in a time frame that feels comfortable. When you get busy and caught up in daily life, self care may slip away and this Sleeping Naked After 40 Guide may be put aside under the growing pile of things that need your immediate attention. I am suggesting a few options for you to create your own schedule for change. On your calendar, mark the dates and deadlines (such as you would for a very important appointment or commitment with someone special) indicating when you will finish each chapter. Now of course the only penalty for missing the date is the toll it will take on your body and your health. I almost never show up unexpectedly at your house to smack some naked sense into you. But I guarantee that something WILL happen when you do finish in the committed time.

For starters, you will feel amazing at having completed a task you set out to conquer. Completion will also prove to you that a life of extreme self care and love is not as difficult as you previously thought; it is actually do-able. How's that feel? Pretty good, right?

Consistency is important. Persistence is imperative. As you learn and grow and form new habits, changing your food and implementing self care becomes easier and less like a chore. Kind of like the first real job you ever had. Remember how overwhelming and impossible it seemed to absorb all that new stuff. Sit with that for a moment and really remember what that overwhelming feeling felt like. Perhaps you thought you'd never learn it all or understand it all, that it was a mistake that you were ever hired in the first place. Now remember how you felt after you mastered the skill and you could perform your tasks and job without even thinking about it. It was natural, a habit, and EASY.

Food is key, not only because we need it to live or because we eat at least three times a day. Food can be your friend, your enemy, your nemesis, your crutch, your drug, your joy, your fear, your struggle, but ultimately food's purpose is to sustain life. You have to eat. But when you elevate food beyond the grab and go of a chaotic life, mostly eaten when standing at the sink, watching TV, or grazing your way through fast-fat drive-thrus, to a more spiritual practice requiring thought and preparation, things change. Your practices of filling up, stuffing down, overeating, or overdoing convert to healthy, nourishing, and you begin the art of nurturing your beautiful body. That's when the magic happens. Take a moment to sit with this concept.

Describe your relationship with food in just one word.

_____

Mine used to be "challenging".

Okay so back to the magic that is yours for the asking. Magic, yes; a snap of the fingers, no. You are the magician of your own life, and if you've ever met a magician, they will tell you how much practice it takes to perfect an act. So remember - patience, persistence, commitment and some "work" are at the core of your success.

Check one option that works for you:
☐ One lesson per week, taking twelve weeks to complete.
☐ One lesson per month, taking one year to complete.
☐ Read through the whole book before you decide on either of the above in order to familiarize yourself with the material. Then go back and select the best way for you to absorb the content and complete the exercises.
☐ Your own way/timeframe (If you chose this one - remember WRITE DOWN your consistent, sensible plan.

_____
_____
_____

Taking whatever time period you choose, go ahead and mark your calendar and mark your completion date with weekly or monthly dates; this way you are scheduled to devote time and attention to reading your lesson. Treat it like any other appointment you would be required to keep. It is important that you maintain consistency (without stressing) and dedication (without becoming overwhelmed). This is your program; fall in love with the idea of falling in love with your amazing self.

Remember that the purpose of your journey is for you to:
- Increase your confidence so you can do anything
- Achieve your ideal weight that is sustainable
- Improve your health with more energy and happiness
- Develop new, sustainable, implementable skills
- Change your life as you fall in love with your naked food and your naked body
- Be able to look in the mirror naked and full on and love what you see!!
- Ultimately feel sexy enough to SLEEP NAKED in confidence and pride.

The "naked" information that I share in my guide is different from what you will read in other books. I have a unique way of sharing my golden nuggets and little jewels. This treasure chest (book) is jam-packed with them. You can simply open to any page as a daily reminder and pick out a new thing to focus on. Sometimes all you need is a little SMACK to knock the self care into you. Other times you will need more guidance and a clearer picture of the road ahead. You personally play an integral part in how this program maps out. You will incorporate an implementation plan to track your success and sustain changes. The steps must be followed until they become a habit that works for you and is "styled" into your life. By no means am I saying that practice makes perfect. Because we all now know that there is no such thing as perfection, right? Once you get that out of the way, you have nothing to beat yourself up about. Isn't that just plain ole' freeing? No perfection to freak out about. WOW! **It's time to be okay with being I.M.Perfect.**

What matters is that you do your absolute best in any and every situation. When doing your best at any given period in time, you feel good. Realize that your best will always be different; it may not be 100 percent, 100 percent of the time. And that's because situations may, understandably and momentarily, change our resolve, but they should not be used as an excuse for repeatedly lowering your expectations. For example, if you work out when you're tired and have an injured shoulder, your best will be different than when you are well rested and in perfect health. The way you enter into your workout session will be the same each time—striving to do your very best under the circumstances. This is the best advice I can give to you for alleviating any disappointment in yourself. (**THIS IS SUPER IMPORTANT!**)

Sit with this new concept for a moment: why do anything at all if you are not doing it to the best of your ability? Here's my opinion on this: don't do it at all if you can't give it your best shot, because by shortchanging yourself and the experience, you will be plagued by failure and never, ever realize that you can do it. But give it your best shot with a dose of grace built in and you'll see shifts, changes, discoveries, uncoveries and a new way of being. (If you think I sound like someone's mother, the fact is I am so it's hard to shake off that role in life! But I want for you what I want for my kids - a happy, healthy, amazing life.)

Let this mother (be nice now) take your hand and show you, step-by-step, how to plan and implement strategies that you can easily incorporate into your daily routine. Together we will be the catalyst for change.

> *"If you want to change your life, you've got to change things in your life."*

This stuff is do-able. I am not making this up. I know it is doable because I do it. I've had private clients tell me that it is do-able; the recipes, suggestions, tips, and ideas all work when you actually do them. One said, and I quote, "Rosie's menus are super easy....totally healthy...amazingly gorgeous.....sexy body guaranteed!" Woo Hoo!"

I get it; I know you are busy and overwhelmed. You have a list of things to take care of, and your own name is carelessly scribbled on the bottom of the list. How do I know this? I wrote this book because although I had read tons of books, none of them took me by the hand. I was sick of books that overwhelm readers with information overload, and no clear way to implement their plans on an individual basis. I want to help make it easy for you to learn how to implement and sustain a new way of eating, living and thinking about yourself.

> *"Remember that even tiny little changes produce enormous results".*

This is an experience. Each of us is a work in progress; consistently improving and growing. Think of yourself a lump of clay. You may even be feeling that way right now as you start this journey. But clay can be molded and shaped into any form by its artist. You are the artist of your life. How cool is that for a visual? What shape do you want for yourself? You can create that.

I revisit my Personal Development Plan (referred to as Grow Yourself in Lesson 8) regularly and make changes that make it easier for me to succeed. Consistency and follow-through are stepping stones to success. You can expect changes to occur if you participate fully in the process. To implement and sustain a new lifestyle you've got to figure out what works with your life. I prefer to call it "styling your life" to support a healthier version of yourself. You need to consider: your job, family structure, taste preferences, eating preferences, timeframe, and body type. The plan must work for you. Think about the ridiculously simplistic reasoning behind that. If it doesn't work and FIT into your life, then you ain't gonna continue doing it. So figure it out and make it work. It's that simple. Make changes along the way; note when you slip up and consider how you might reduce risk if it happens often or just accept the fact that "Hey, it happens", then quit kicking yourself over it, and get back on track as soon as you can.

> *"If the changes you make don't FIT into your life, you are not going to stay FIT"*

Even though you may be excited and motivated to change your body and life for the better, rushing like a mad woman to change overnight will not work. It will, in fact, work against you as you will inevitably QUIT when the going gets tough and burn out sets in.

Self care is about being kind and gentle with your beautiful self. Don't be invested in the outcome, or interested in why you can't. Just take the small, implementable steps one at a time and the changes will happen.

The easiest way to do this is to focus on one meal at a time - the one in front of you, and, make it count. It means not counting the calories but making every calorie count.

> *"Don't be interested in the outcome or invested in why you can't."*

What I Want For You

For good or bad, physical appearance is the first thing we notice about a person: we are both judged and judge others on appearance. I want you to be the best that you can be in your physical body—healthy, sexy, and at your ideal weight, at any and every age and stage—so that you have the confidence to do everything that you want. When you are "Sleeping Naked" you are comfortable in your body and in love with yourself. Practicing self-care and self-love perpetuate weight loss and increase your confidence and self esteem.

My mission is to inspire and motivate you to fall in love with yourself, your food, your body, and your life. When you need support, motivation, a loving push, or a gently shove in the direction of your power, think of my voice whispering in your ear (okay, sometimes shouting in your ear): "You can do this." It is your right as well as your obligation to take extreme care of yourself.

> *"You always CAN, if you want it bad enough."*

Remember, YOU are worth the extreme care that I prescribe throughout this book. You are worth the time and effort that it takes to create your very own Personal Development Plan and Grow Yourself as you build your healthiest, sexiest body. Are you ready to fall in love?, with yourself? your food?, your body?, and change your life forever? Of course you are.

(Moving) FORWARD

This is your "twelve-step guide" for developing the confidence and courage to fall in love with your food, your body, and your life. These twelve lessons break down components into "do-able" pieces — **focused, sustainable, implementable changes, one step at a time, one meal at a time, and one day at a time.**

You will be taken down a path of twists and turns (partly because I am an extremely creative multi-tasker with ideas that pop up randomly, that I am excited to share. Top that off with a dose of ADHD-ism, and you've got the twists). I don't like labels (either on my food or to describe the being that is me. I mention ADHD with love, and only as a reference for you to understand a bit more about the nature of the author and where I am coming from).

Each transition, adjustment, and exercise is connected and intertwined with the others. Embrace the fact that you may not absorb it all at once. You will pick up different gifts at different times. There is no right way or wrong way. Your sponge is unique; the way you learn is your way, and it is okay. Your goal is to get it—soak up each lesson, tip, idea, and story, and make it work for you.

Let's go, engage and have fun.

Lesson Breakdown

Each chapter of Sleeping Naked after 40 is set up similarly and includes a Topic Title, Naked After 40 Vocabulary Words (so you can understand the lingo as you read along), and three sections:

• **The Nutrition Transition** (Get your body in the game)

and know what the frig' you are eating. This topic looks at how you are currently eating and helps you create alternative ways of looking at your food—what, when and how to eat.

• **SMACK** (Get your head in the game)

and lose the "baditude". A SMACK is my endearing term for a wake up call, ouch, jolt, smack, two by four or sledge hammer adjustment in your attitude that prompts you to think outside of your current behaviors, opens you up to the idea and possibility of change. Your wake up call encourages you to lose the baditude you have been touting and become a bad ass in your thinking! With a shift in your thinking, you can do anything you set your mind to.

• **The Experiment Experience** (Get your heart in the game)

and actually "do" something specific (I think of these as mind experiences and experiments) that will help you to think differently, shift your awareness and give you a different experience to build upon. Dig deep and face your emotions instead of eating them. Read, acknowledge, participate, and complete the exercises at the end of each lesson to create your own unique experience. This is important, because it is only through experience that you gain the assurance and confidence that you can do it. Once you have done something once; the second time is always easier.

These experiences are discussed at the back of every lesson. This is your book, so feel free to write, journal, doodle in it. I have added an additional section, "Experiment with the Experience Section", in the back of the book so you can have a place to work and write. You purchased this book, which means you are open to (and looking for) change. Your awareness that something needs to change is your first step toward healing and health. I invite you to participate fully in this process. Some of it will seem easy; some of it will be more challenging. Please honor wherever you are in your journey, but understand that for it to be most effective, you need to commit.

I am sharing with you a program of routines and practices that work for me and countless clients who have made amazing changes in their food, their bodies, their way of thinking, and ultimately their lives, and as long as you are "all in" and participate fully then you'll get all the information that you need , when you need it, right out of this book. Each lesson will end with a rose. When you complete all twelve chapters, you will have earned a dozen beautiful roses. I recommend you make it a habit of treating yourself to real flowers to brighten up your home and your heart after completing each chapter. Reward yourself for doing a good job.

The Set-Up

You may be stressing that the lessons haven't started yet, although you are excited to dive right in. That would be like diving into a swimming pool without ever having had swimming lessons. I am deliberately slowing down the process here to make sure you are focused and understand what is expected. That's why I call this the set-up. The more prepared you are, the more you'll get out of it. I want you to be open to getting it all—and you will, if you have patience. This also serves as a mini test; if you don't read every page it demonstrates that you are willing to take short cuts and are focused more on the outcome than the process. And that could interfere with your success.

Remember, it's not about how much you know; it's about how you act upon what you know. The power lies in taking one simple step at a time. Get up for a minute, stand at the bottom of your staircase, and look up toward the top.

Can you see the top step?

You may see it, but you can't get up there in one big leap, can you? You have to first take a step and then keep on taking steps. Those steps will eventually get you to the top. You can take the steps as quickly as possible or as slowly as you desire. **But remember you cannot get to the top without those in-between steps.**

This step-by-step process focuses on sustainable and implementable changes that will help you build a healthy, sexy body, one you are comfortable living in. These changes are designed to support and push you as you learn the skills that work best for your life "style."

"Style" is being comfortable in your clothes and your own skin. It is falling in love with yourself and projecting that love in all you do. You do it by developing the habit of feeding and treating yourself with "extreme self-care." And by this time you should know that extreme self-care propels you to fall in love with yourself, with your food, with your body, and with your life, so that ultimately you are comfortable and confident enough to sleep naked.

If you are in a rush, I suggest you slow down. If you are still in a rush, go ahead and charge the stairs and take two chapters at a time. Be cautious, however, because the faster you rush, the more likely you are to slip up and fall. I suggest taking one step at a time. Master that step, be secure on that step, and move forward to the next step only when you are firmly planted and balanced. You are your own best judge; go with your gut and do what you feel will work for you.

On the subject of slipping and falling, let's be real: you may reach a point where you think you screwed up. You may fall off. You may get frustrated. You may even want to flex your towel throwing muscle at me and revert to your old habits when you are faced with a challenge that seems unbearable at the moment. Remember, there are no real mistakes. Mistakes are lessons and learning. It's cool if you rephrase and look at it from that perspective. When you are off, you're just off, and there is no need to make it into more than that. Being all in and committed doesn't mean you won't screw up. Being all in and committed does mean that you will change and grow over time as the cumulative effects build, and that's when the magic happens.

Whichever way you choose to ride, enjoy it; make it work; and just DO IT. You'll be watching with wonder and amazement as your food changes and your body transforms. You'll witness how you create the life of your dreams by caring for and loving the gorgeous, sexy YOU.

The Commitment

(This is your commitment. Read each statement as "I"…cuz it's all about you, baby!)

Let's commit to a better life. Fill out, sign, and copy your commitment letter below. Make a copy and hang it in a prominent spot on your refrigerator or bedroom mirror as a daily reminder that you come first. Shocking, right? Take this part seriously. Whatever you put into your lessons is what you are going to get out of them. Remember to fill in your calendar with your completion dates. Nothing gets accomplished without your participation. Shocking, right?

My Commitment to My Life and Health

Today, I have chosen to start improving my life by letting go of the weight that has been weighing me down. I commit to Sleeping Naked After 40 and learning new steps and techniques for loving and taking extreme care of myself and my body by changing my food and my attitude.

I will give 100 percent commitment to myself.

I understand and accept that this is a process, a journey, and a life lesson, and that it may feel uncomfortable and challenging at times. I commit to pushing through with consistency, persistence, and sheer determination to make these changes that will improve my life.

I honor and love myself enough to give myself the gift of health and extreme self-care.

By participating in Sleeping Naked After 40 , I understand that I am learning, growing, and experiencing how to eat differently by nourishing my body with pure, natural, naked foods, and that I am becoming aware of how food can improve my mood, self-worth, and confidence.

I understand that this program is not something that I can start and quit. Rather, it is a step-by-step growth process that is sustainable over time and has the ability to change my life for the better, forever, as these new ideas and routines become habit.

What I learn cannot be measured on the scale, and I enter into this contract with myself with an open mind and open heart. I will listen and give opportunity to adopting and adapting new and different ideas, tastes, and experiences, persisting with those that work in my life and my improved lifestyle.

My dear body (your name goes here),

After careful consideration and thought, I make the following commitment to continually strive to:

1. Prioritize selfcare
2. Honor you as the place that holds my soul
3. Nourish you with pure, naked, healthy foods
4. Realize that it is my obligation to keep you healthy
5. Love and appreciate you for all that you do for me
6. Accept that I have the power to make changes that heal you
7. Exercise regularly and appropriately for you
8. Listen to the messages you send to my "gut"
9. Continually replace my old story and negative thoughts with new, productive, positive ones
10. Let go of toxic foods, people, and situations that are holding me back from being my best
11. Be grateful for all that I have and less focused on what I don't have
12. Put on my lipstick and dress myself as the beautiful, sexy, confident woman that I am.

(Add any additional commitments and intentions that you have)
_____
_____
_____

Love xxooxx, Me. (your name here)

The Inspiration: Strength Beyond Muscles

I got my body in the weight loss game by personally losing 38 pounds in 4 months. I got my head in the game when I made a commitment to a specific goal. I got my heart in the game when I decided to put myself first with self care and love, and do whatever it took to reach that goal. I became less interested in distractors and focused only on what I wanted and flexed the strength I possessed beyond my muscles. Presenting my best self (which by the way I presented on stage, nearly naked!) changed my life and the lives of other women as they become inspired to present their best selves. My story started with a desire and a decision.

It was my life-long dream to participate in a body building (figure) competition. But I got sidetracked by family responsibilities that distracted and consumed me. Approaching 50 challenged me to take a naked look at **ME**. Could a forty pound, overweight, out of shape, overwhelmed, 50 year old mother of three, become a figure (bodybuilding) competitor?

Inspiration came from my adult children who suggested I stop talking about it and just do it, and my own disgust at feeling fat and frumpy. I set a goal and made a decision to commit 100% to fulfilling my dream. I put blinders on, earplugs in, thanked the

naysayers and saboteurs and took the steps one at a time! I wanted to compete with my 20 year old daughter at my side, but our chaotic schedules collided. If we were to do this together, the only possible competition was a skimpy 16 weeks (4 months) away. I was challenged and determined to learn what I could do for my body in that time so that it would serve me well when we stood on stage, pretty nearly naked!

Our goal to pose next to each other forced me to focus, work really hard, and lose the weight that would prevent me from confidently taking the stage. I gained amazing life lessons as I realized my inner beauty was there all the time. I simply created a more beautiful package in which to carry myself by first starting to care for myself in more loving ways through better nutrition and food practices, consistent exercise and letting go of stuff that was no longer useful in my life, like carrying around unwanted heavy weight.

Jaws drop when people see the photos of me with my daughter. A friend suggested I had "strength beyond muscles" and it was that inner strength that unleashed my real power, possibility, inner beauty and strength beyond muscles.

Lessons I learned in this competition continue to inspire me and now I am inspiring other women to be the best that they can be. Through this deeply personal discovery, I help them create their own healthy, sexy body to house the beauty that is within.

Make no mistake about it, I am by no means trying to turn you into a body builder. I offer support and ideas for you in building your best body and best version of yourself. Only you know what that looks and feels like. Fall in love with the idea of "building" your best self and presenting that "self" to your life "stage" and the world.

In order to play in this weight loss game, you've got to have 3 pieces to the puzzle and they are not only diet and exercise. They involve your body, your head and your heart. So let's get started; You gotta play to win..

Now let's "rock" your world..

LESSON 1

Naked After 40 Vocabulary

Choice:
The determination of the mind in preferring one thing to another. Good to remember that not making a choice is still making one.

Control:
You may not have control over the crap that goes on around you but you do have control over the crap you put in your mouth.

Courage:
The ability to stand up and go for what you want, even when you feel fear. The willingness to persevere, even when your little doubting thoughts and sabotaging friends suggest that you can't. The power you innately possess that enables you to go and get what you want, because you know what you want.

Confidence:
The belief in your abilities and recognition of your own beauty and power. The only real accessory you ever need to look and feel like a rockin' hot, sexy woman.

Change:
The result of what happens when you combine all of the above.

Baditude:
Negative nonsensical made up stories of disparaging thoughts that get you nowhere, such as snide, unfavorable, scornful, disdainful, crappy thoughts about yourself, your body, and your abilities .

Bad Ass:
Formidable, Excellent.

Let's get real about your body.

You only get one, and it's an awesome one. You are an incredible machine and a walking miracle. Have you ever thought about yourself as a walking miracle? I mean really, think about the things your body does. Lots of the amazement happens naturally without your conscious effort. There are so many things we take for granted. Consider your health - your body's natural state. When you are not cooperating with your body by not treating it very nicely, making poor food choices, or engaging in poor self care habits, it politely lets you know by sending you a wake-up call (or a smack). You know what I mean. You get so tired you can't function, you get rundown, you get a belly ache, you get a cold because your resistance is low. "Hello!" a message from your body to your brain. It's not so politely telling you, "What about me? Can you give me a little attention, please?" Maybe this book called your name as a wake-up to start you on the self care process. Maybe your body nudged you on the shoulder and was either gently whispering or angrily shouting as you stood in front of the mirror, telling you that something is just a little out of whack.

It amazes me how much we, as human beings, don't know about our own bodies. We study them, a little bit in school, a little drawing here or there, but hell, it's not the focus. Half the time, we aren't even using our most important life force that supports our very existence - our breath! Notice how many times you catch yourself holding that breath. Stop for a moment and notice that now. Where is it coming from? Where is it going? Is it deep? Shallow? Slow? Fast? Are you holding your breath?

Your amazing, awesome machine is incredible and capable of so much. Some of the things your body does, like losing 50 -100 hairs from your head everyday and replacing them the same day, happen without your participation. (I take that back, you may notice the falling out part in your bathroom sink). Personally I did notice that the hairs grow back but I find them in the most inopportune places, like my chin. OY! (and, I also noticed that no one ever warns you of this over-40 phenomenon or talks about it and it'a a pretty amazing feat). However, there are many bodily functions that occur naturally as our way of healing and regenerating. Here are just a few of the interesting things that your body does that I can't resist sharing. These super cool facts will bring proof to my suggestion that your human body is one smart and resilient cookie (or maybe a carrot is a smarter thing than a cookie).

1. The heart pounds with enough pressure that it can squirt blood over 35 feet.

2. In 30 minutes you give off enough heat to bring half a gallon of water to a boil.

3. Every single person has a unique tongue print, (as well as a unique finger print)

4. We shed about 60,000 particles of skin every hour. (that's about 105 pounds by the time you are 70 years old)

5. Your nose can remember about 50,000 different scents.

If it does this much without your conscious help, imagine how much more effectively your amazing machine will run when you fuel it properly with nutrient-dense foods that support your body's ability to flourish.

I'd be remiss if I didn't mention the WEIGHT thing, the other trapping that women are capable of shedding, besides skin. Women are also very capable of finding it again, very quickly! Bet you have your share of experiences in the lost and found weight department.

Research shows that the average woman goes on 2 diets a year or about 104 diets throughout her adult lifetime (between the ages of 18-70). That can add up to spending 10 full years on a diet. For at least one in ten women, that number skyrockets to about 25+ years of a women's life on a restrictive diet. I was one of them.

Where do you fit in? Whatever the number, it's too much already and it has to stop. So much struggling around this issue is not good for your soul. It's a diversion from the more important, profound, fun things you can be working on in your life.

But it's not just enough to say "Okay, I am not dieting anymore, so I'll just resign myself to the fact that I hate my body". Your weight affects your health first and foremost, but your weight also affects your self esteem. That is the reason for Sleeping Naked After 40. Your self esteem is inherently connected to how you feel about yourself and how you present yourself in this world. You might try denying it but it is true.

> *"Increased self esteem will not only help you sleep better, it will help you do everything better."*

The extra baggage you carry in the form of weight is heavy and may be stopping you from being social, from trying something new and exciting or fully living your life. You may be stopping yourself from doing certain things until you get to that "skinny" weight you dream of as the ideal. I know you know what I'm talking about. If you are not living your life to your full potential, then in no way are you being the best mother, best friend, best wife, best girlfriend, best worker, best sister, best daughter, best you that you can be. How are you showing up in your life and in the eyes of the people around you?

_____
_____
_____

Take a moment, and think about yourself. What are you missing out on by not being comfortable in your own skin?

_____
_____
_____

What would change in your life if you felt better in your body?

_____
_____
_____

What are you currently doing that you know is sabotaging you from being at your ideal weight?

_____
_____
_____

How is this extra weight affecting your self image and confidence?

_____
_____
_____

What is this added weight holding you back from?

_____
_____
_____

The key, the solution, the answer, the gift, if you choose to accept it, is to stop right here. To accept that wherever you are right at this moment is the perfect place to be.

"AHH?" you say. "Really? But you just said I shouldn't adopt the belief that I am stuck here?"

By accept I don't mean resign yourself to staying at your uncomfortable, unnatural weight or state of "unhealth". I don't mean give up and stay where you are. I mean surrender and stop struggling. I mean that NOW, at this very moment, you begin acceptance of and love for that magnificant physical form you call your body. After all, it is where you live. If you saw that your house was getting messy and decrepit from neglect, wouldn't you want to straighten it out? But with our bodies, there's no option of moving out of the neighborhood, we have to improve the home that will be with us always. If you start the process of falling in love with the idea of building the best version of yourself without starving, beating yourself up for "mistakes" and spending hours working out, the whole journey will be fun. Remember how great it felt the first time you fell in love? How about having that feeling about yourself? Your resilient body is willing to forgive you your past mistakes (so your mind should, too) and become a better version of itself with each of the smallest changes you make. The extreme self care process begins right now – make the choice to move toward a more fulfilling life. Once you start this process, everything will fall into place. (Even those annoying saddlebags you may be carrying)

"So how do I even begin?" you ask.

The best place to start taking care of your physical body is to pump it up with better fuel in the form of nutrients. Start to nourish yourself with pure, naked food. "Pure, Naked" does not mean boring. They are not one and the same. Kick (or smack) that old myth to the curb.

Start with "Pure Naked" and you start to feel better and as a matter of fact you start to feel amazing. Need another reason to start? This combination of choice and the feeling of control it creates results in your resilient body showing up as its most glorious self.

NUTRITION TRANSITION (Get your body in the game)

Careful Choices

So next on your "To Do" list (after making the choice) for your extreme self-care practice is to make careful/thoughtful food choices. How do you do that while being so busy, and stressed and overwhelmed with other areas of life?

One meal at a time, ladies, one meal at a time. I love my one meal at a time mantra because it works. It keeps you focused and right in the here and now. You can stop thinking long term thoughts of when will the diet end and when will you get "there". Every meal presents another opportunity and chance to improve your health. This is another case where the tactic sounds too simple or like I am harping on a single issue. But imagine for a moment making every meal the best it can be? (by best I mean healthiest choice for your body given the time and circumstances going on around you.)

> "When you eat crappy food (aka: nutrient deficient processed garbage), it shows up on your body; when you eat pure and naked food, the body of your dreams show up".

Become aware and accept that it does matter what you eat, and that unhealthy foods (processed, refined, fake foods) are going to have an adverse affect on your health including but not limited to making you fat. Who needs it? I stopped thinking about counting calories, dieting, or depriving myself when I embraced this concept. It may take you a little practice, if you've had years of "diet" immersion and lessons in eating for weight loss. You know, the fake, low cal, low carb, low usefulness food. You can stop labeling yourself in terms of "good" and "bad" depending on what you ate. (Besides, I hate labels; did I mention that before?)

Change how you use your words and thoughts.

> *Stop thinking about what you can't have and start to focus on what you can have.*

Stop dieting to lose weight, and reprogram your focus on your health. It's much easier to pass up on the unhealthy food options when you are making the choice based on your HEALTH and how you are going to feel after you eat it. I know that I feel like crappola after eating sugar. I have the experience of not being able to function on the days after sugar corrupts my system. So with that knowledge comes the awareness that sugar caused it and then I can make the choice to stay away from what is technically poison to my system. Staying away from foods that don't make me feel good is not deprivation; it's a skill for living in a healthy state. And more importantly it's my choice to pick how I want to feel. And why wouldn't I want to feel good and gorgeous all the time?

Nourishing your body with pure and naked foods is not at all complicated. You don't even have to know how to read labels. I discuss this in more depth in "Cooking Naked After 40", the cookbook that goes along with this healing journey. The premise is identifying and using food as close to its natural state as possible. Food is absolutely linked to the way we feel; it dramatically affects our moods, our behavior, our energy, and our attitudes.

> *"Food is absolutely linked to the way we feel; it dramatically affects our moods, our behavior, our energy, and our attitudes."*

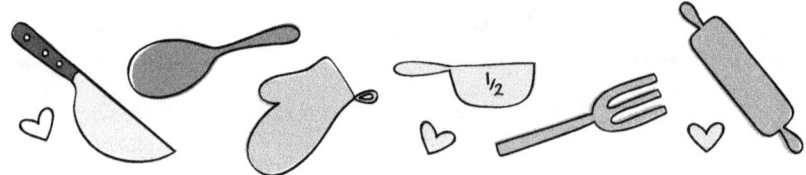

YUM. NAKED RECIPE:

STRAWBERRY ALMOND DRESSING

Here is a simple naked dressing recipe that takes only 3 ingredients and only 3 minutes to make. It is not complicated or cumbersome but can yield exceptional feelings of yum-azing proportions.

Ingredients:
- 1 cup strawberries
- 3 TBSP almond butter
- 1 TBSP balsamic vinegar

Directions:
Mix this in a powerful blender (like Vitamix) and get real!
You'll never have leftovers of this yummy, gorgeous real food recipe. You can drizzle this pink delight (it's so pretty in a glass bowl) on your green salad, top off a bowl of oatmeal, dip in some celery, carrots, asparagus, chicken, eat it straight up with a spoon, or even freeze it for a cool summertime treat!

> *"When you choose each meal—every day—by making better choices, your mindset will change, your eating style will change and your body will follow."*

SMACK: (Get your head in the game)

You Choose

Stop being a negative, nonsensical nilly. Not only do your food choices matter, but your attitude is a major contributor to losing weight and feeling great. I call it a "smack" - a wake up call, a brain shift, an "ouch", that propels you to lose the baditude you may be carrying and replace it with bad ass thinking. With a shift in your thinking, you can do anything you set your mind to. If you are already saying, "This seems too hard; who's gonna do this; I'm not giving up my sugar", then SMACK! You have an attitude adjustment to make. Changing your mind (attitude) will change your life.

I am going to share a personal family story of motivation to demonstrate how attitude plays a major role in producing results. My daughter played sports for 16 years, excelling in basketball since she was five years old. She was always the star player. She's now twenty-one and plays at a competitive college level. I watch her every day, working and fighting for her playing time on the court. She eats right, works out hard, practices often, rests properly, and does the things she needs to do to increase her chances for success.

> *"Lose the baditude and become a bad ass instead!"*

My daughter explained to me that this was the first time in her basketball career that she was not the best and strongest player on the team, her first time as a "bench kid" as she called it. I imagined this must be the hardest thing for her, so I was shocked when she explained that being a "bench kid" was really kind of easy. What she meant was that it is easy to become complacent, easy to get comfortable with simply accepting that this is just how things are going to be, and even easier to make excuses about how it is everyone else's fault but your own. It is so much easier to live up to your status as the "bench kid" than to try to disprove the label. To get off that bench…now, that's the challenge! She decided to work hard every day, even when the voice in her head said, "Why work hard? You'll always be the bench kid." She made the choice that it was important to her to get off that bench, and that's what she did. No magic involved, just a change in her attitude—a recognition of where she was and what she had to do to get where she wanted to be.

> *"Changing your mind (attitude) will change your life."*

So what's the label you've been carrying around? You may be the fat sister, and you may have always been the fat sister. Just because you were doesn't mean it always has to be that way. You can change your body. At this point it may be easy and comfortable to accept that branding. Maybe you've even labeled yourself as an "emotional eater". Get rid of the old name tag, remove that badge from your chest and create a new handle for yourself. Make it one that feels better to hold onto. Let's begin by changing these "bad" attitude titles to "bad" ass instead. If you were labeled in the past as the fat sister, well that was then, so what? Now what can we change that to? How about re-titling yourself as the "most voluptuous of the bunch"? People pay big money for voluptuousness. Savor that instead of the fat. If you were labeled as an "emotional eater", that title no longer serves your needs today. Re-title yourself as an "emotional feeler". Now that feels better, doesn't it?

If the changes you want to make in your life seem hard, they probably are. But it's up to you; you can choose to take the path of least resistance and just stay in that rut..

That's probably fine with everybody. But is it really fine with you? Are you happy sitting on the sidelines just because it's easier, or are you ready to do the work that it takes to get off that bench?

EXPERIENCE EXPERIMENT (Get your heart in the game)

Get Off the Bench

What is your bench, (your situation), and what negative myth have you embraced that keeps you on the bench as a second string player in your own life?

_____
_____
_____

How do you think it would feel to get off your bench?

_____
_____
_____

What is stopping you from living up to your full potential? (Examples: accountability, support, time)

_____
_____
_____

How does it benefit you to stay where you are? (Not sure this needs more than one line – but I'll give you three just in case you're more attached to your bench than I guessed.)

_____
_____
_____

Is the thought of being your best a little scary? Why? What would happen if you were in the best shape of your life right now?

_____
_____
_____

What small step are you not taking that you know would be moving you toward improved health?

_____
_____
_____

What would change in your life if you were living up to your full potential? List three things.

1. _____
2. _____
3. _____

What will the date be one year from today? Write that date down.

_____

If, on that date, you were what you consider your "best physical self" and in your "best physical body," what would your life look like? Describe in detail.

_____
_____
_____

Sleeping Naked After 40

{ List 3 changes that you will implement in your life after reading this lesson:
1. _____
2. _____
3. _____

You've earned a rose.

LESSON 2

The Morning Attitude

Naked After 40 Vocabulary

Practice and repeat:
Practicing new healthy tactics and repeating them so that they turn into healthy habits.

Bars and jars:
Unique recipe ideas that are quick and easy and leave you no excuses.

The Morning Attitude

The lessons in this book are building blocks for getting stronger and developing the tools for building a healthier, sexier body. Just like a house needs a strong foundation, to build a healthy life, you need a strong foundation. Changing your unhealthy actions into healthy habits is a great place to start. As your habits become healthier, you become stronger and stronger, and it becomes easier and easier to build upon what you have already learned. The more you learn and change, the easier it gets. As you begin your new lesson, keep in mind (and keep in practice) what you learned in the previous one. Continue to take notice of everything you put into your mouth and how it makes you feel. Remember that you are in control, and the choice is always yours when it comes to what you are eating—and what you are thinking.

Mirror, mirror on the wall… Who the heck is that looking back at me? Have you ever had this feeling as you looked in the mirror? Maybe you woke up one day—and were officially fat!—and realized that the noticeable effects of eating too much of the wrong things had transformed your body into an alien image you don't want to see. If that's your wake-up call, be grateful and wake up!

A woman from my 30 year high school reunion, we'll call her Becky, approached me and said, "Hi, remember me? It's me, Becky; I'm in here under all this fluff." She had gained over one hundred pounds since high school graduation. That feeling of "it's still me in here", "hiding under all that fluff" can hit you in the head one day and wake you up (smack). If you are fortunate, the hit will be caused by an upcoming event like a reunion or wedding, where you want to be seen looking your best. At worst, the wake up call can be a life threatening illness or the threat of having to go on medication for the rest of your life. Whatever the reason, the work to be done is looking back at you from the mirror. Use the wakeup call with gratitude as it may be the catalyst that moves you to action. It may be the very thing that makes you promise yourself that you will never look or feel this way again. It may make you realize this is the worst you ever looked, and you will only look better every day from here on in. I have a friend who thinks this way when she has a cold or the flu – she waits anxiously for the day she feels the absolute worst, happy in the knowledge that she will only feel better every day after that supposed low point, so she's grateful when she reaches it.

> *"Last time I checked, there were no rules that said frumpy, fat and over forty go together."*

Changes happen slowly over time. Maybe you gained back the weight you worked so hard to lose, or maybe you are out of shape and get out of breath while walking up the steps. Either way, forget about how you got here, and focus on what you are gonna do about it now? How are you going to make this time different?

There could be a horde of conspiring culprits that helped you along your path…a dead-end job, a toxic relationship, a chain of unfortunate events, lack of fun and joy. The end result is the perfect storm of misery that sinks your self-esteem and floods your life with doubt. These struggles show on your face and in your body. Being overweight and out of shape is the outward sign that things in your life are messy and "weighty". At that point it becomes a painful and arduous chore to get dressed in the morning because nothing fits or looks good on your body, and that messes with your mindset, your attitude, and confidence in a big way. By the time you should be ready to leave the house, you are ready to throw in the towel, or forget it all and bury yourself under the covers to hide. See I told you "I get it, I've been there"….and you should know I can help you get out of that vicious cycle.

What are you willing to do to make things different?

_____

_____

If your body is out of shape, and you are carrying around the burden of extra weight, you may be thinking, "I can't do this, it seems so overwhelming," or "I've tried and nothing works." Are you going to allow negative self-talk and baditude weigh you down further? "I can't do this again." "It's too hard." It's too much work." "I don't' have time to eat healthy." "It's my hormones." "It's my age." Blah, blah, blah. They all sound like excuses to me. This negative self-talk can turn into a self-fulfilling prophecy. You can leave your excuses in the last diet book you read. Not here. This is not a diet book and you can do the simple steps that it will take to yield big results toward a smaller you.

My choice to enter my bodybuilding (figure) competition was not to focus on the weight loss (although that was a nice part). It was to prove to myself that I could do whatever it took to be the best that I can be. I took this goal and put systems in place, set my life up to succeed, and made the changes that needed to occur for me to reach my goal. This happened by recommitting my focus every single day and making each the best day that it could be. Breaking it down even further, I made each meal and each workout the best that it could be.

We have this one precious life, and if we are not happy and loving every moment we have, everything we do, even every ounce of food we eat, we are cheating ourselves and everyone else that is touched by our life.

It's amazing to me how many people go off to work each day, hating their job, their coworkers, and their boss. They do the same thing every day, hating everything they do, but thinking it's the only option that they have. (Jeez, I sure hope that's not you). They focus on how it will be when they hit retirement age and get out of their jobs. And so they plan for that distant future. I would call that wishing your life away. Thirty-two years ago, I was working in a bank in New York City, under fluorescent lighting (that made me sick), in a square cubicle (that made me sick), in a corporate environment (that made me sick). I went to work every day (that made me sick), and waited for lunch so I could get outside, get away from it, and then I waited for the end of the day so I could go home. I realized I was "waiting" my life away and enjoying nothing. That job did not last long; soon I realized that I needed and wanted to work exclusively with people, thoughts and an environment that I loved. I made my life's goal never to work in an office again.

> *"Waiting for the right time could result in "waiting" your life away and consequently enjoying nothing while you are waiting."*

Are you going off to a job you dread? Are you wishing your life away, day by day?

Negative thinking brings more negative thinking, and it just keeps piling on until we are so stressed out that we can't see our way to feeling better. We get stuck in a rut, and we become incapable or unable to find a way out.

There is a way out: step off the hamster wheel, and start with your attitude. Start building bigger and better attitude muscles. Similar to building muscle by working out with weights —exorcising the toxins out of your mind and spirit takes consistency, persistence, and time. Whenever a negative thought pops into your head, thank it and let it go. Replace it with a positive statement. Your body can only think one thought at a time. So why not make the thoughts you think good ones. Good thoughts feel so much better and you deserve to feel good.

Good food, good thoughts? Woo Hoo!

Here's a little food for thought. Your attitude and thoughts are directly affected by the food you put into your body. Uh oh, what does that say about us? There is energy in the food you eat and it affects you both physically and emotionally. The food you eat gets digested and becomes part of you. It travels through your blood stream and your body to your organs and into your cells. It therefore makes sense that it must impact your brain and your thoughts. I guess that means we literally are what we eat. If you eat crap, you then think crappy thoughts and oh ya, you look like crap.

> *"Your attitude and thoughts are directly affected by the food you put into your body."*

NUTRITION TRANSITION (Get your body in the game)

First Meal Matters

Your first meal matters. Eating breakfast and starting your day in a nutritious way has an immediate impact on how you feel for the rest of the day. If you are already in the habit of eating breakfast, that's good news. We'll explore how you can make it healthier. If you are not eating breakfast, you may need to reconsider your decision!

Time to 'fess up to your excuses for skipping breakfast…..

Is it that you just don't feel like eating when you get up?

Are you rushing around like a madwoman the second you step out of bed and can't seem to find the time to get to the breakfast table?

Are you short on ideas of what to eat to eat so you opt for a "pretend to be healthy fake whole wheat" bagel? (aka: infested sugar carb bomb).

If you answered yes to any of these questions, some simple lifestyle adjustments are needed.

Take notice of how skipping breakfast makes you feel? After going without food for eight to twelve hours while we sleep, our bodies need to break the fast and refuel for the day ahead. Think of your body as a fireplace. If you stop adding wood to the fire, the fire will burn out. Your body's metabolism is the process by which the body converts the fuel in food into energy. You need to refuel yourself in order to get your metabolism up and burning.

Breakfast can help keep your weight in balance. When the metabolism gets fired up with fuel, the body starts burning calories. Studies show that people who don't eat breakfast often consume more calories throughout the day and are more likely to be overweight than those who skip lunch. Mood and energy can drop by midmorning if you don't eat at least a small morning meal. That's because if you skip breakfast, you are more likely to be starving by lunchtime, and make bad choices based on the warped messages your body is sending in its deprived state. You have to fuel your willpower with pure naked food or by midmorning you won't be able to stop yourself from lingering outside the conference room hoping to nab a left over bagel or muffin or stalking random strangers carrying big boxes of donuts, offering to get them a platter so you can surreptitiously stuff one or two honey dips in your mouth in the process, or you'll find the fastest clock in the building to give you permission to leave early so there's no line at the all you can eat lunch buffet. (No, of course, I'm not talking to you! hee hee)

Not only is it important to have breakfast every day, but what you eat in the morning is also crucial. A healthy breakfast should consist of a variety of foods, such as whole grains, protein, and fruit. Experiment with your breakfast. Try mixing different food groups and see what works for your body. You are unique—what works for me may not work for you. One thing that does work for everyone (and every body) is pure, naked food.

Fruits and vegetables. There are many varieties and colors to choose from.

Grains. Hot or cold whole-grain cereals, sprouted grain breads, or leftover grains from dinner.

Healthy Fats. Nuts, seeds, nut butters, avocado, salmon.

Protein. Eggs, nut butters (peanut, almond), wild salmon, nuts and seeds. The point is to fall in love with your good health and the foods that promote it.

Greens. Yes. I did say greens! These babies are powerful for breakfast. Now you may find greens hard to grasp (for breakfast) but they can be yummy delish. Take a few romaine lettuce leaves, sprinkle with avocado and a few nuts, sprouts, seeds and roll it up. You've got a super duper energy packed breakfast.

Notice that there are no refined boxed cereal, cakes, muffins, bagels on this list.

We are creatures of habit, and you will find that you are most likely eating the same foods over and over. Have some fun and experiment a bit. When you find a few healthy breakfast options that you like, you can stick with them. It will be easy to get them ready to go during what may be a chaotic time of day.

Breakfast is my favorite meal. I don't do anything without completing my breakfast routine, sitting down at my table and eating what I love, lovingly. After years of working with clients, most will tell me that breakfast winds up being their fave as well. But that truly comes after they have experimented with exciting new options and graduated from grabbing a bagel to mixing up a bowl of oats and berries.

> *"Stop eating cake for breakfast. It will set you up for a sugar fest day!"*

If you are eating a breakfast that lacks nutrition and is loaded with sugar—woe to anyone who gets in your way! Sugar can make you tired, angry, moody, and unproductive. Most Americans start their day off with dessert - in the form of sugar-laden carbs like huge bagels, muffins, donuts, pastries, and sugared cereals.

If this is you, I am glad you are reading (and hopefully) digesting what I am saying. If you are caught in this bad habit, you can transition to healthier options, and you will fall in love with the way you feel after you start eating better. This is a great opportunity to make your mind/body connection: notice how you feel after a donut and cup of coffee versus oatmeal with blueberries and a cup of green tea.

This is a great time to experiment and try some exciting quick, easy, and nutritious breakfast options you can find in the breakfast section of my Cooking Naked After 40 "Create, Concoct, and Cook Book".

Since each body is different, it's useful to conduct a personal breakfast experiment. It allows you to see which healthy foods feel good in your body, and it also provides the opportunity for you to experience that what you put into your body does matter.

What is your favorite breakfast now?

_____

_____

How can you adjust your schedule to make time to eat breakfast?

_____

_____

But wait—there's another huge benefit to eating breakfast: it will help you start your day off strong! If you make your first meal a healthy one, chances are you will feel empowered to continue that trend throughout the day. Each meal counts toward your goal. It's also a great way to feel taken care of. For this, my favorite meal, I eat out of my favorite red (made in Italy) bowl, and I make the best oatmeal ever! I use steel-cut oats, which I soak overnight to cut down on cooking time in the morning. (I save lots of time by putting the oats and water in a pot and bringing them to a quick boil at night. Then I take the pot off the stove, cover it, and let it sit overnight. By morning, it only needs to be heated for about three minutes, and it's perfect!) I add a variety of toppings and make my first meal of the day a real treat. My choices on any given day could include a mix of the following: walnuts, bananas, cinnamon, coconut butter, flax, blueberries, cherries, almonds, apples, raisins, dates, almond milk, quinoa, peanut butter, sweet potatoes, and pumpkin. It's like my oatmeal is a wonderful taste surprise every day, and it's yummy delish!

Did I mention that I sometimes sprinkle organic, 70 percent cacao chocolate chips on my oatmeal, where they melt on top? YUM!

I get hungry just thinking about it! Can you tell yet that I love my food? You will, too! The best part of eating pure, naked whole foods is that they not only taste good, but you feel so much better than when you are weighed down with a big white-flour bagel bomb. I tell clients that they might as well just take a roll of tape and attach that bomb to their waist, because that is where it's going to show up eventually anyway. The "bombs" blow you up. Just wait to see how you feel after eating an awesome breakfast. Try something new and let me know what your favorite oatmeal combo is. Email me at rosie@sleepingnakedafter40.com.

> *"Be patient. Over time, your taste buds will adjust to a healthier way of eating and you'll fall in love with how "naked" foods taste."*

There's no need to add brown sugar. Just because you used to eat your oatmeal that way, does not mean you should still be doing the same thing when you now know the detriments of sugar. Your taste buds are super duper smart and friendly and they are very open to change and the opportunity to experience new things. If you are trapped in that "oatmeal-needs-brown-sugar syndrome," you can transition slowly by using less and less each day, and see what happens to your taste buds. Or you can try gentle sweeteners like honey, pure maple syrup, or stevia, which are much easier on your system and will help you transition from refined sugar. Give yourself a week or two, and you won't even miss it! Be patient. Over time, your taste buds will readjust. They'll get healthy for sure.

> *"You are one smart "naked" cookie when you trust your gut and really allow yourself to listen to your taste buds."*

There is no acceptable excuse you can come up with for not having the time to prepare a gorgeous morning meal. If you are now thinking, "Rosie, you're nuts; I don't have the time to make oatmeal", I can take care of that for you. No, I am not going to show up in your kitchen and cook for you. I am going to tear down every excuse you can put up. Here are 2 separate and fun ways to eat your oats, easy and easier.

Pick your fave.

Since our society is obsessed with bars, I choose this oatmeal bar as a healthy alternative to store-bought items. It's simple, naked, pure, and will only take you twenty minutes to whip up and bake. This is one snack that I call make 'em, freeze 'em, grab 'em when you need 'em. You will see a lot of this type of recipe suggested in this book because it's all about making it easy for you.

> *"The best healthy eating plan is the one you actually do."*

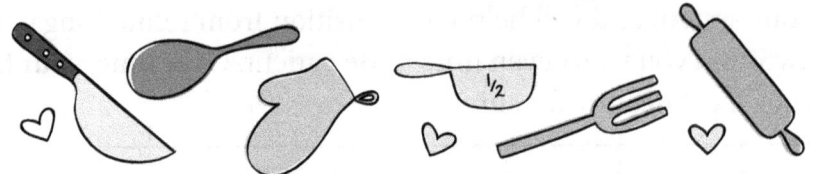

YUM. NAKED RECIPE:

OAT BARS

- 4 ripe mashed bananas
- 1 apple (shredded with cheese grater/skin on)
- 1/2 cup pure pumpkin puree (not pumpkin pie filling) or left over sweet potato
- 4 cup rolled oats
- 1/4 cup shredded unsweetened coconut
- 1/2 cup chopped walnuts
- 2 TBSP flax
- 1/4 cup pumpkin seeds
- 1/2 cup raisins

Mix wet ingredients into dry ingredients and press into a large 9 x 11 baking dish. Bake at 350°F for 20 minutes or until firm. Let cool on counter and cut into 2 x 4 inch squares. Freeze individually and wrap in little baggies. There you have your oatmeal in a bar—and no more excuses for not being healthy on the run.

If you are not into baking and are getting ready to tell me that time is your issue, you can stop right there. I can suggest another option that is so quick you'll run out of excuses.

YUM. NAKED RECIPE:

OAT JARS

For a No-Excuses-in-the-Morning, Easy Oats Breakfast

- 1/4 cup regular oats, uncooked
- 1/2 cup unsweetened almond milk
- 1 TBSP chia seeds
- 1/4 ripe banana, peeled and smashed
- 1/4 tsp pure vanilla extract
- 1 TBSP flax

Directions: Mix ingredients together in a mason jar (or you can use a leftover glass peanut butter jar). Cover and place in fridge overnight.

In the morning, top with ten chopped almonds and 1/2 cup berries. It looks like a parfait and is fun to eat right out of the jar!

What are **chia seeds** and why should you eat them?

Chia is the Mayan word for strength. It is an ancient superfood that is touted as a mega-energy food. Chia is perfect for you "naked" busy ladies who need added energy to get all your good stuff done. You want to eat this beautiful food, as it has 2X the protein of any other seed or grain, 5X the calcium of milk, 2X the amount of potassium found in bananas, 3X the antioxidant strength of blueberries, and 3X more iron than spinach. Need I say more? Okay, I will. I'll also tell you that it provides energy, boosts strength, bolsters endurance, levels blood sugar, promotes weight loss, and aids intestinal regularity. If you've been stuck (ahem) it'll make you go.

> *"You can't go back and change what you ate for breakfast yesterday. So what will you do differently today?"*

SMACK: (Get your head in the game)

It's All In Your Attitude

Anything worth having is worth working and waiting for. Since negative thinking brings more negative thinking (and pulls negative things) into your life, it may be time to change how you think about things. Negative thoughts are toxic and can make you sick, much like toxic and unhealthy foods make you sick.

How do you start to change your current way of thinking to become more positive, and consistently thinking better thoughts about yourself and your life? Replace the old with the new. Just like you are replacing bagels with oats, replace bad thoughts with good ones.

Just a little FYI, you are awesome, no matter what you weigh or what job you have or what situation you are in. You are awesome. I know this for certain. You've got to trust me here.

It's time to adjust your baditude and give yourself a break. You didn't gain your extra weight in one day, and you are not going to lose it in one day, either. Treating yourself with a little patience and kindness is what you need to do right now.

Let us practice a new way of speaking to yourself. Write down this little mantra/prayer and tape it wherever you will see it throughout the day. Practice daily and repeat often:

I am awesome. My weight is not a reflection of my value. It's simply a measurement for the moment. I choose this day to make every moment count. I will take care of myself and do everything to the best of my ability, including feeding myself with good food and good thoughts.

> "Stop beating yourself up…all mistakes are necessary lessons, and all screw-ups are wake-up opportunities."

You've got to stop being so mean. Seriously! If you spoke to a friend the way you speak to or about yourself, would she stay your friend? Highly unlikely. So stop it. (smack)

I started to switch my thinking by focusing on the simple idea of becoming my own best friend. When I did that, I became kinder and nicer to myself. I didn't beat myself up, because I would not do that to anyone else, especially a friend as special and fabulous as me. I would show my friend love.

If your best friend who you love a lot "screwed" up big time, small time, or just did something considered "not so perfect", what advice would you give her?

_____
_____
_____

What kind words of inspiration, understanding and support would you share with her?

_____
_____
_____
_____

I might tell her that it's okay to make a mistake, because that's how you learn. I might tell her to pick herself up and get back on track. I might offer to help with kindness and patience. I might remind her that she needs to be patient and persistent with what she wants to accomplish and that over time, with little baby steps, she'll get where she needs to go. I might remind her that I love her as she is, and that she is perfect for today. And here's what I wouldn't do. I would not buy her a hot fudge brownie sundae or take her out for marathon margaritas, because that would be like salting the wound as well as her glass rim and adding another layer of crap to her already crappy day. My objective would be to support her through the rough patch with healthy and helpful friendship, advice (if I had any) and activities. I might stock up her pantry with some healthful goodies knowing that she might be tempted to make bad choices while feeling a bit low, so I'd want to help her by making good choices easier.

If you are living a healthy lifestyle—eating well, moving your body, and taking time for yourself—these food changes and lifestyle changes will show up in how you look and feel. They go together. Be patient, be consistent, think health, and the changes in your body will come along naturally. It's what you do most of the time that makes the difference.

Speaking of differences, your baditude makes a huge difference in your ability to change what is not working in your life. When you begin to notice the good in every situation, instead of the bad, seemingly insurmountable goals become surmountable. If you set your mind on something, you can achieve it! If you believe you can achieve it, you will achieve it! This is what I would tell her (my bestest friend), and this is what I will tell you.

> *Switch your thinking by focusing on the simple idea of becoming your own best friend.*

EXPERIENCE EXPERIMENT (Get your heart in the game)

The Breakfast Menu Experiment

This experiment is about discovering what works for your body. Try these different breakfast foods and complete the chart to discover how you feel right after you eat the food and how you feel three hours later. How does eating differently in the morning affect your food choices for the rest of the day?

Breakfast Food	How I feel right after eating	How I feel three hours later
a large bowl of cut up fruit		
plain ole' oatmeal		
oat bars		
oat jars		
deli bought muffin with coffee		
eggs and toast		
other:		

Your body is unique. Listen to your gut and trust it. Your body will let you know what it wants, if you just listen.

Notice, listen, feel, be aware. What's your favorite breakfast and why?
_____
_____

$\left\{\begin{array}{l}\text{List 3 changes that you will implement in your life after reading this lesson:}\\ \\ 1.\ _____\\ 2.\ _____\\ 3.\ _____\end{array}\right.$

You've earned a rose.

LESSON 3

Cheers to Sleeping Naked

Naked After 40 Vocabulary

Affirmations:
The positively positive voice inside you that pledges and declares that you can do, be or have anything you set your intention on.

Unlimited potential:
The limitless power you possess once you get out of your own way.

Bulletproof:
The idea that the strength you possess toward fulfilling your dreams is impenetrable.

Cheers to Sleeping Naked

We all have our own idea of what it means to be "healthy." When polled, 9 out of 10 of my clients agreed that WEIGHT was the one thing they would change about their health. The consistency of the response spanned every kind of amazing women in many different situations, stages and shapes, from extremely successful entrepreneurs to loving, caring, giving moms and every combination. The point is, we woman are very attached to our bodies (in more ways than one) and how we look and feel in them. Sometimes we observe from a distorted view and sometimes we refuse and resist self love and self care.

Here are ridiculous statistics from other womanly polls. Reading them makes me realize that, ladies, we are crazed and need to take some control back over our bodies and our self worth. We need to change these statics by owning our power, and using our love as a base of our confidence our happiness with our actual self, not just our ideal self. One at a time, let's move out of these stats and into a life of joyfully accepting, acknowledging and transforming our bodies and our attitudes (mindset or headspace). Note that the bolded letters at the end of the stats are my comments, and sorry, but, I just could not stop myself from commenting in bold type.

Stats!

"An average US woman is 5'4" tall weighing 140 pounds; the average US model is 5'11" weighing 117 pounds!" **No friggin' way!**

"44% of US women are on a diet" **Oy vey!**

"80% of US women do not like how they look" **Oh my!**

"A total of 109 MILLION DOLLARS is spent in the US every day on diet and weight loss products' **Sad!**

The stats are not mine (they are from (www.eatingdisorders411.com) but the comments definitely are!

Weight is the one area of our health where we should (seemingly) have the most control. And, yet, we don't. Since our weight is attached to the type and amount of food we consume and the only thing between our hand and the fork we hold in it and our mouth and the food we put in it, is our head, then it reasons that our HEADS/MINDS must be controlling our ability (or inability) to lose the weight we say we want to lose. Want to know something else pretty shocking… 9 out of 10 women polled said that they KNOW what to do to maintain their best body weight; they just don't do it. Well, girlfriend, there's a straight line from A to B so where are you veering off track, hmmmm? What's preventing you from being the best you can be?

> *"The only thing between our hand and the fork we hold in it and our mouth and the food we put in it, is our head"*

Do you know what to do but can't wrap your habits around doing it? What's up with that? How is it that you are so smart you can multi-task with the best of them, create beauty in the world, run a business, and raise fabulous children, but when it comes to this topic, you can't seem to get right?

Everyone knows the key components of building a healthy, sexy body are food and exercise. Even if you haven't adopted the principle yet, you know you are what you eat and you know that if you are not moving it, you are not losing it. So again, what's up with not being able to do what you know you need to do?

Let's make a deal. Let's make a real deal. Your desire to get healthy has to turn into a decision to do the things necessary to change your life. SMACK!! Ouch, wake up call, jolt, slap, bang, boom. The key is in your head.

> *"Your head and heart must jump into the game and join your hand and your mouth."*

A small little component of permission will add to this practice and give it the fuel it needs. Along with food and exercise comes the permission to take some loving caring time for you.

Okay, I get it. You have your list. And everyone else is on it but you. Everyone else ranks. You've got these things you've got to do. You've convinced yourself and now you are trying to convince me just how impossible it would be to take some well deserved personal time. Since you are over 40, you were raised with the idea that if you take a moment for yourself, it would be perceived as a selfish act and heaven forbid someone thinks you are a self indulgent, spoiled brat. I get this, too.

But let's do the math. Humor me here and divide 60 by 1440.

4 percent.

How can it be possible that with 1440 minutes in a day, you can't even grab 60 of them for yourself? Really?

Park your boatload of built-in excuses as to why you can't take an hour a day for yourself and leave it in the ocean to wash away with the next wave, never to be seen again. Doesn't that feel cleansing?

I am going to give you a gift right now. If you refuse to use it, I will be insulted, so do me a favor and participate and make me happy. This is a gift you are supposed to use because it works and as you get familiar with how time with and by yourself feels, you will never miss a day in your life.

PERMISSION SLIP - This slip grants the bearer PERMISSION to spend 15 minutes a day doing whatever her heart desires. There is no excuse or reason good enough to stop this mission. This slip entitles bearer to no guilty after effects.

PERMISSION SLIP - This slip grants the bearer PERMISSION to spend 15 minutes a day doing whatever her heart desires. There is no excuse or reason good enough to stop this mission. This slip entitles bearer to no guilty after effects.

PERMISSION SLIP - This slip grants the bearer PERMISSION to spend 15 minutes a day doing whatever her heart desires. There is no excuse or reason good enough to stop this mission. This slip entitles bearer to no guilty after effects.

DATE:
What I did with my permission slip:_____
_____

It felt _____
to have some rockin' hot fun for myself.

DATE:
What I did with my permission slip:_____
_____

It felt _____
to have some rockin' hot fun for myself.

DATE:
What I did with my permission slip:_____
_____

It felt _____
to have some rockin' hot fun for myself.

This pink slip officially fires you from your self-appointed position of having to do it all. Whew! Let me hear a collective sigh of relief as you realize you are now free from that impossible role and have moved up to the number one spot on your list. Don't rationalize or dwell on this. Just do it.

As a healthy, sexy, gorgeous rockin' hot woman, you are entitled to and responsible for your own self care. There are 1440 minutes in a day, you are encouraged and allowed to use 15 of them for just you. (I am not even insisting on the full 60, yet, I am talking about only 15 minutes for now. You can do that!) Exercise does not count. You must do something frivolous, silly, fun, different, exciting, exhilarating, untraditional, sexy, unique or you may just do nothing at all. You may not, however, harbor any GUILTY feelings, whatsoever. It's a pink slip, it's not a choice. It is a condition of living your good life.

So what can you do in only 15 minutes. Here are some suggestions to charge up the frivolosity brain cells you've been neglecting.

> 1. Mellow out, ladies!
> Light some candles and sit quietly with yourself, by yourself and enjoy the company.
>
> 2. Dance like nobody's watching.
> Put on your iPod and hit the disco library (this is not exercise; it's a joyful release of energy).
>
> 3. Lookin' Hot Hot Hot.
> Flip through a sexy fashion magazine for the stylin' hot outfits you want to (no, make that will) wear.
>
> 4. Destination Imagination.
> Cut out pics of exotic and simple places you love.
>
> 5. Chronicle your fabulous self with a "Look What I Can Do" chart….
> Number a paper from one to ten and have at it, get beyond the mental block and identify your strengths.
>
> 6. Express yourself. Draw/color/paint/haiku.
>
> 7. Mash up some modeling clay and restructure it to your heart's content.
>
> 8. Unpolish for a more polished look.
> Take off your old chipped nail polish.

Next, another list - Jot down 5 things that you can do that would be silly, fun, different, exciting, exhilarating, untraditional, and out of the ordinary for you. And if you giggle coming up with the list – that's a good thing!

1. _____
2. _____
3. _____
4. _____
5. _____

NUTRITION TRANSITION (Get your body in the game)

Drink Up

While you are using your pink slip to increase the joy in your life. Slip some watering habits into your day for hydration and for health. Both "slips" are necessary to improve your state of health and happiness.

The experts offer an easy way to calculate how much water you need, equating it to drinking half of your body weight in ounces. This usually means approximately 8–10 glasses of water a day. Okay, maybe that's not so easy; think of it this way – if you weigh 160 lbs, you should drink approximately 80 ounces of water. There are 8 ounces in a cup so divide 80 by 8 and voila! The answer is 10 cups of water per day. And you thought you'd never use math after high school! (Math-phobes – just pour yourself a pitcher of water that includes 8-10 cups and sip on it throughout the day until it's gone.

Though I should especially be on board with this since I've made a serious occupation about knowing what to do for good health– I admit that I have a big list of personal excuses for not drinking my water. Allow me to share what were very boring excuses. I don't like to drink cold water in the cold weather. I don't like to have to run and pee all the time. But here's the difference, I drink it anyway because I am committed to my healthy, sexy body. In fact I developed some helpful and fun ways of getting the water that my body needs. But first, here is a flood of water information.

Since your body is made up of about 75 percent water, every physiological process that takes place in your body, including fat burning and muscle development, depends on it.

Water is necessary to:
- regulate your body temperature
- transport nutrients
- build tissues.

Water aids:
- proper digestion
- circulation
- respiration
- nutrient absorption
- and excretion.

So here's the deal. You need to understand exactly how important water is, so how about a few more facts:
- your brain is 90 percent water
- your bones 22 percent water
- your blood 83 percent water
- and your muscles 73 percent water.

Are you ready to drink up??

What if you knew that water:
- supports your metabolism
- protects your joints and bones
- and detoxifies your body?

Thirsty, yet?

Let me share my watering secrets with you, and you can come up with your own. What you do matters less than that you just do it. And hey, even if you already love drinking water, you may just need some cooling ideas.

- Carry a bottle in your purse and car.
- Keep a bottle of water by your bedside at night and drink it up before you even get out of bed in the morning.
- At dinner, serve your water in a beautiful wine glass. Drop some raw cranberries into the bottom of the glass. So pretty!
- Prepare warm tea by bringing water, fresh ginger, and cinnamon sticks to a boil in a pot. This makes a soothing tea water.

- Add a splash of natural, unsweetened fruit juice to your water (cranberry, grape, orange). I personally use stevia for a sweet treat.
- Guzzle (yippee) a glass of water before every meal; that will help fill you up and therefore cut down on the quantity of food you eat.
- Carry a water bottle wherever you go. Try www.kleankanteen.com for environmentally friendly, virtually indestructible, reusable stainless steel canisters. They come in all sizes.
- Keep ten ponytail bands around the bottle and roll them up or down as you refill the bottle and consume the water throughout the day.
- Try adding sliced cucumber to your water and let it sit for a bit. Delish!
- My fave: Drop a teaspoon of goji berries into your water and squeeze fresh lemon. The goji will plump up and flavor the water slightly, and you'll get a fun little chew every once in a while.

Making a gradual change in drinking water will allow you to develop a taste preference for it in a short period of time as well as a ritual around including it in your life. Do whatever works for you to get this process woven into your lifestyle.

You'll feel great! Think of yourself as a plant that has just been watered and brought fully back to life.

Sometimes, when you feel fatigued, it's actually because you're dehydrated. Often, when you think you're hungry, you are really just thirsty.

Drinking more water will help you to drink less soda and juice.

YUM. NAKED RECIPE:

OH...CINNAMON

- 6 cups water
- 1 inch of fresh ginger peeled
- 2-3 cinnamon sticks

Place all ingredients in a pot and bring to a boil. Your house is going to smell yummy and your tummy is going to feel good.

Oh—and I am sorry to be the bearer of this news—your alcohol, your wine, your coffee, or your tea cannot replace your clean pure naked water.

"Keep your Eating SIMPLE and keep your Cooking NAKED"

- Add a splash of natural, unsweetened fruit juice to your water (cranberry, grape, orange). I personally use stevia for a sweet treat.
- Guzzle (yippee) a glass of water before every meal; that will help fill you up and therefore cut down on the quantity of food you eat.
- Carry a water bottle wherever you go. Try www.kleankanteen.com for environmentally friendly, virtually indestructible, reusable stainless steel canisters. They come in all sizes.
- Keep ten ponytail bands around the bottle and roll them up or down as you refill the bottle and consume the water throughout the day.
- Try adding sliced cucumber to your water and let it sit for a bit. Delish!
- My fave: Drop a teaspoon of goji berries into your water and squeeze fresh lemon. The goji will plump up and flavor the water slightly, and you'll get a fun little chew every once in a while.

Making a gradual change in drinking water will allow you to develop a taste preference for it in a short period of time as well as a ritual around including it in your life. Do whatever works for you to get this process woven into your lifestyle.

You'll feel great! Think of yourself as a plant that has just been watered and brought fully back to life.

Sometimes, when you feel fatigued, it's actually because you're dehydrated. Often, when you think you're hungry, you are really just thirsty.

Drinking more water will help you to drink less soda and juice.

YUM. NAKED RECIPE:

OH...CINNAMON

- 6 cups water
- 1 inch of fresh ginger peeled
- 2-3 cinnamon sticks

Place all ingredients in a pot and bring to a boil. Your house is going to smell yummy and your tummy is going to feel good.

Oh—and I am sorry to be the bearer of this news—your alcohol, your wine, your coffee, or your tea cannot replace your clean pure naked water.

"Keep your Eating SIMPLE and keep your Cooking NAKED"

SMACK: (Get your head in the game)

Affirm It

As our bodies need water to hydrate, function and perform well, we also need to water down the pesky negative thoughts that creep into our psyche. This is necessary for our health and balance.

Pre-created self-affirmations that inspire, motivate, excite, and push you forward are necessary tools to have in your good health box of tricks. They act as little reminders, encouragements, and support—and we can all use some of that.

You have the power to create a statement about who you are, your potential, and what you want to happen in your life. The more you repeat these positive affirmations, the more they become part of your thought process.

Affirmations are stated in the present as if they already exist in this moment. This allows you to experience the feeling as if you were already living that potential. With practice, these little positive self-truths become easy to create. Invent them for different situations that occur in your life—when you need added support, motivation, a reminder of your worth, or encouragement. When you need to crowd out the negative self-talk, these positive affirmations are a great replacement. The more you repeat them, the more they become a part of you. When the negative talk pops up, push it aside and replace it with your better self-affirmation. Your mind cannot focus on a negative thought and a positive thought at the same time, so replace all Negative Nellie's with Positive Penelope's.

It's pretty easy to create an affirmation – try this exercise:

A "who you are" affirmation, which represents your real self, what and who you are, can begin with "I AM…."

Your "unlimited potential" affirmation, puts forth your true potential, and will have powerful implications. You can begin with the words: "I CAN….

I created a self-affirmation, which I wear on my bracelet, so I can look at it often. I will share it with you as an example of what you can create for yourself. It states:

I AM POWERFUL. I AM STRONG. I LIVE MY GIFT.

It is a reminder to me that I can do anything I set my mind to and that I live my gift of inspiring, motivating and educating women to be their best self.

What do you want your "who you are" affirmation to remind you of?

_____
_____
_____
_____

Create your affirmation here:

"I am…" choose the words that speak to you. If you get stuck, ask yourself if you are creative, unique, friendly, giving, loving, caring, sensitive?

_____
_____
_____
_____
_____

If you are having trouble putting words together, try one of these:

- I am perfect for today.
- I am beautiful.
- I am healthy.
- I am my perfect weight.
- I am confident and in control.
- I am smart.
- I am sexy.
- I am creative.

- I can do anything.

…and on and on and on. Do you get it now?

Confirm your "unlimited potential" affirmation:

I can… _____

_____

_____

_____

_____

_____

_____

Louise Hay is an author who started speaking way back in 1976 before it was fashionable to talk about the mind and body connection. Her healing techniques and positive philosophy are still helping millions learn how to have better lives by using their own thoughts. Her basic premise is that "Every thought we think is creating our future." She offers wonderful CD's on affirmations and power thoughts. Check out these inspiring CD's at www.louisehay.com.

There are many leaders out in the "thought" world and you can pick and choose the one that is speaking your language. You'll know it when you hear it; so experiment and feel who's speaking to you. It's as easy as putting a CD in your car, and while you are driving, sip your water and purify your body and your mind with positive, beautiful affirmations, and begin to retrain your brain. This is one of many steps we will be taking as we begin our journey toward treating ourselves with the kindness and respect we deserve.

> "Watch your thoughts; they become words. Watch your words; they become actions. Watch your actions; they become habits. Watch your habits; they become your character. Watch your character; it becomes your destiny" ~Frank Outlaw

If this affirmation process is not feeling right for you, go slowly. Relax and breath. It will take hold over time if you keep it up and keep a consistent pace; you have all day now, don't you?

You can also think of it a different way. What if every time you're in a "not-so-fun" or unhappy situation, you think about others in worse situations or consider how your situation could have been worse than it is? This little trick puts things in perspective. It's never really all that bad. You know what "they" say about putting your problems in a pile with everyone else, you will always choose your own problems over someone else's.

EXPERIENCE EXPERIMENT (Get your heart in the game)

Make and Tape

Here are some suggestions for focusing on your affirmation/mantra/positive thoughts/improved thinking.

- Write it down.
- Tape it up to your refrigerator, mirror, and/or treadmill.
- Put a copy in your wallet.
- (My fave) Make a beautiful beaded bracelet. (They sell inexpensive bracelet-making kits at craft or bead stores. This is a fun project that can serve as a creative outlet for you; perhaps a great way for you to use your pink permission slip). I wear my bracelets proudly every day, and they serve as a reminder. I have tons of them. Depending on what mood I am in and what attitude I need to shift, the bracelet affirmation reminds me to focus.

Here are the bracelets that I made with rose quartz crystals and beads reminding me of strength and persistence. While I was training for the competition, there was a popular song that was always on the radio, titled "Bulletproof." Working out  one morning, my daughter told me that the song reminded her of me because, she explained, I was bulletproof and she made me a bracelet to match. Feel free to have fun with your words, and be open to the words and phrases that flow to you. When I wear my bracelets, I just have to know they are there and feel them, and I feel empowered.

If you don't want to make a bracelet, designate a piece of jewelry that you already own. You can even wear a rubber band on your wrist (not too tight please) as a reminder of your affirmation and commitment to yourself. Whatever works and whatever you can find the time for is what you should incorporate into your life. Everyone is different in their approach so find what speaks and works for you in your life.

Lather, rinse, repeat. I often wondered what the heck they were talking about on that shampoo bottle. Why do you have to repeat the washing process? Wasn't one time good enough? Apparently it is helpful for us to repeat over and over that thing we are attempting to relearn. That new repetition becomes a new habit. Repeating your affirmations embeds them in your brain, much like a video or a song that replays over and over. Subconsciously, you hear it, you feel it, you believe it.

When you wake up in the morning, repeat your affirmation to yourself twenty-five times in the mirror and again before lunch and before dinner and in the evening before bed another twenty-five times. It's helpful to pull it into your psyche when challenged with an issue. What you are really doing is retraining your brain to think and respond differently.

List the places where you will place your motivational affirmation (your mirror? your refrigerator door?):

_____
_____
_____

What and who can possibly stop you now?

(Your correct answer should be: "Absolutely nothing can stop me now." If this is not the answer that pops easily out of your mouth, practice it until you believe it—or, as my mom used to say, "Fake it 'til you make it."):

_____
_____
_____
_____
_____

List 3 changes that you will implement in your life after reading this lesson:

1. _____
2. _____
3. _____

Buy yourself a flower or a rose as you complete lesson three to remind yourself that you are beautiful.

LESSON 4

Greens Clean and Clean Leans

Rosie Battista

Naked After 40 Vocabulary

Get real:
Using your knowledge to make choices to pick foods that are pure and naked and as close to their real, natural state as possible.

Come clean:
The art of cleaning up your act—what you eat and who you hang out with—getting rid of toxins that weigh you down physically and emotionally.

Go green:
The ability to change how you think about eating. Make the meat the treat (less), and make the salad the main meal (more)

Greens Clean and Clean Leans

Greens clean your gut and clear your mind—detoxifying and energizing! Greens make you happy; I kid you not. They act as little antidepressants, giving you energy and a mood-enhancing experience. Eat them at each meal, and you will see and feel the difference. While some foods give you instant gratification that lasts mere minutes, greens will keep you happy for a lifetime! Remember that speech in the movie "Wall Street" where Gordon Gekko (played by Michael Douglas) says "Greed is Good"? Think of how much better things would have turned out if he'd believed instead: "Green is Good"

Surprise! In this lesson, the focus is on eating your greens and, of course, cleansing your body from whatever "toxins" ail you. Let's face it: we all have our own personal food demons tempting us.

NUTRITION TRANSITION (Get your body in the game)

Eat more greens

Green is the newest, latest, greatest, coolest way to participate on this earth. Everyone is looking for the greenest way to participate and keep the planet healthy. Believe it or not, going green with your body, by eating more greens is the best way to keep your body healthy.

There is no instant solution but there is a nearly magic pill to weight loss, increased energy, vibrancy, disease protection, and health. The prescription reads – "eat more dark leafy green vegetables." Sure, there are supplements out there that are "green". However, they don't call them "supplements" for nothing. By definition, a supplement is "something that completes or enhances something." So what is that something? It is eating the green stuff in the form of a vegetable.

Let me make a formal introduction to my friend, kale, one of my favorite vegetables, so you can familiarize yourself with it and build your own intimate relationship. Kale is yummy delish and can be eaten raw or cooked.

> *If there were a magic pill for weight loss and health, in my book, it would be kale. Steam it, boil it, bake it or eat raw.*

I'll be honest, kale used to scare me. I was like WTF is that? The only vegetables I knew were broccoli, corn, peas, and carrots. Overcooked mushy ones, I might add. The only thing I knew about kale was that it had nice curly leaves and was a great, cheap way to decorate baskets and buffet tables. But that was then, and now, I am like a reformed smoker. I have to try to remember I used to think kale was for decoration only. And now when people say that to me, I cringe. Most of my clients wind up with kale being their fave. If you tell me you don't want to try kale, we are gonna have a problem. I will not so politely try to convince you of the benefits of this glorious leaf.

If I can't convince you, I'll implore you to become BFF with this amazing stuff. At least try some kale chips. You will feel my passion and become passionate about kale, too. The stuff is downright addictive once you start. I am quite sure it's your body's way of reminding you that it wants the good stuff, the yummy stuff, the healing stuff. No matter what ideas you have about kale now, once you experience this stuff, you'll never want to leave it again. Never heard of it? Don't feel bad. Kale doesn't have the marketing team of Fritos to create brand awareness. And, hey, as they say, you don't know what you don't know until you know it. And now you know: kale rocks.

The ANDI (Aggregate Nutrient Density Index) is a chart for the rating of a food's nutritional richness value created by Dr. Joel Fuhrman. Dr. Fuhrman is a medical doctor, (and a man I deeply admire), who believes that nutrition is the prescription for health and eating to live). Guess where kale ranks in the ANDI scale- kale earns the highest rating at 1000. Only one other vegetable scores 1000 along with kale and that is collard greens, another amazing dark leafy green. These two powerhouse greens are packed with phytochemicals, health benefits, nutrients, and power that hasn't really been fully explained in standard nutrition books. (If you'd like to learn more about nutrient density, check out http://www.drfuhrman.com/library/article17.aspx)

If you are challenged, intimidated, or simply unaware of what to do with these greens, here is the first step: take a deep breath and relax. No stressing over this process. Pretend that I am at the grocery store with you. When picking your leafy greens, think about how you would choose a plant. Select the healthiest, most vibrant-looking greens, judging by color and texture. If the leaves are wilted, flimsy, or brown, walk away. They need to look healthy and gorgeous like you!

In our information overloaded world, you can just "Google it", if you don't believe me about the benefits of eating greens. The truth is that once you start eating dark leafy greens on a daily basis, you'll be amazed and convinced by how much better you feel. Most likely, the challenge that you face right now is not with figuring out that leafy greens are beneficial. After all, most of us have been hearing "Eat your veggies" since we were in diapers. The problem arises when we go to cook them. If kale and collards are new to you, and you are unsure how to make them taste good, just try one easy recipe, and don't be worried about perfection.

Many of us may have heard the argument about raw veggies being a little more nutritious than cooked veggies. Others argue just as passionately on behalf of "cooked" foods.

Let's get you eating a little of both. I believe that our main focus is getting them on our plates—cooked, raw, or whatever. I'll let the researchers and "passionistas" argue it out while I simply do what works best for me. Personally, I love variety, a little of this and a little of that, mix and match. An easy way to do this is to throw some cooked veggies on a raw salad. Or, you can choose your preparation depending on the season; you might prefer cooked and warm veggies during winter and raw, crisp, cold veggies during the hot summer months. I feel like I cover all the bases eating both and all the options mean veggies will never get boring for me.

This chapter was written to inspire you to incorporate veggies in your diet. Read through the tips and ideas and try them, but ultimately it is up to you to figure out the best way for you to move them from the ground into your mouth. Try a new tip; see how it works in your life. Use it or lose it, then move to another. If at first you don't connect with a food, I hope you're always open to revisiting it. Your tastes will be changing. Are you up for the challenge?

Get familiar with your local shopping center. Read labels and look for these familiar green glories:
- bok choy
- kale
- spinach
- collard greens

All of these can be eaten either raw or cooked (includes steaming, sautéing, baking).

Things to keep in mind when on your hunt for the green stuff:

1. Look for "locally grown."(Find a local farmers' market. This is not only fun for the whole family but it is also a great way to support your community and get the freshest produce.)

2. Grocery store organics takes precedence over non-organic foods. (Whole Foods Market has an amazing selection of organic veggies.)

3. Frozen vegetables still count as vegetables. (Any brand will do; however, be sure to read the label for any hidden sauces or salt. They should only contain veggies. I always keep the freezer stocked with some frozen vegetables just in case!)

Tips for adding greenery

- Buy bags of frozen kale, collard greens, and spinach, and store them in your freezer. Frozen vegetables are available at all grocery stores, so even when the fresh produce is looking "wimpy," you've got an option. There is no excuse for not eating your greens. These handy-dandy bags of frozen greens are great if you do not have time to run to the store to restock.

- Sauté garlic, onions, carrots, and mushrooms in a pan. When they are soft, add your bag of frozen veggies and you've got a great mixture. No one will be able to tell they were in a deep freeze.

- Not only are these frozen veggies perfect for emergencies, they are also amazing when added to smoothies and shakes. Spinach is milder in taste; therefore, I consider it a smoothie all-star. If you throw a handful of frozen spinach into the blender with your smoothie ingredients, it will add a chill to your shake and amp up your nutrition value tenfold, not to mention create a beautiful green snack.

- Be innovative! Fresh collard leaves are big, vibrant, and gorgeous. They make a great wrap in which to encase your goodies. You can fill them with a veggie medley, turkey (or any type of chopped meat), tuna salad, or a mixed bean concoction, layer with avocado, tomatoes, and sprouts. Green up your favorite Mexican treat using the collard leaf as you would use a tortilla wrap. It's more nutritious, has fewer calories, and OMG, it's so delicious!

WARNING!

I guess I was not completely honest when I said that eating your veggies has zero drawbacks. The drawback isn't with you, it's with other people. You may be judged and ridiculed by non-veggie eaters! Some people just do not know what they are missing and never fail to throw comments your way. Soak them up and enjoy them, because after all you now have the secret and know the power of the greens. Lucky you.

True story - One morning my daughter and I decided to have breakfast at our local diner. We ordered egg white vegetable omelets with a side of steamed broccoli. The waitress, who became instantly confused and distraught, responded shakily, "Broccoli for breakfast? I don't think we have that". Perhaps with slightly more of an attitude than was necessary (what can I say? I was hungry!), I responded, "So you are telling me that I can order meatloaf at any hour of the day, but you cannot serve broccoli for breakfast?" Of course they had broccoli and honored my request, but it was not without judgment and a small push on my part to get what I wanted. Be prepared to deal with people who think your eating "style" is weird and unorthodox. It takes a bit of getting used to, but because you will feel and look so much better, (and look much younger), it's worth the extra conversation and persistence to get the greens you want. Sooner or later, the people in your life who think veggies are from outer space may even begin to jump on your bandwagon.

We cannot always have complete control over the preparation of our food, especially in restaurants. But remember that you are the customer and the owner is (or should be) happy to accommodate your needs. Do not be afraid to ask and be specific in your request. For example, do not just order a broccoli side dish without a description of how it is prepared (it could be prepared with butter, oil, cheese, deep fried, etc.). Play it safe by ordering vegetables steamed, with sauces on the side, so you are in control. When I cook at home, I have control of both the quality and quantity of the oil I use—and those two Q's matter.

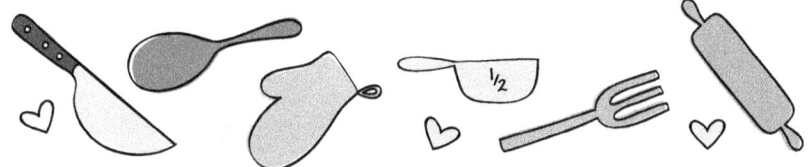

YUM. NAKED RECIPE:

DRESSING THE GREENS

Cashew "Naked" Date Dressing (woo hoo!)
Beyond sweetness and yum-azing!

- 1 apple
- 1/4 cup dates
- 1/4 cup cashews
- 1/3 cup unsweetened almond milk

Combine in a Vitamix and let it spin. Pour onto your colorful plate and enjoy.

YUM. NAKED RECIPE:

If you are nut intolerant, you can try this one

NAKED "RUSHIN'" DRESSING

(and for those who want to whine I can't make something because I'm always rushing, take the two minutes, and with my recipe below you'll indulge in a creamy healthy dressing.)

- 1/2 cup tomato sauce (homemade or check ingredients for sugar-free, without added preservatives)
- 1 TBSP fig vinegar
- 1 TBSP mustard
- 2 TBSP plain Fage 0% Greek yogurt

Mix together and pour on tossed green salad.

This is my gorgeous Vitamix that has been making my life and food better and performing well for over eighteen years. It's a complete nutrition center that takes over your kitchen. It can replace most other appliances, like mixers, mashers, food processors. You'll make space on your counter, and leave it out, as this baby does it all.

In this lesson, you have been formally introduced to two of my most treasured friends and support system: gorgeous, strengthening kale and strong, powerful Vitamix. Both are amazing, and both are necessary for creating health. I hope that you accept this invitation to explore and get to know them both on an intimate level by inviting them into your life and to your kitchen table. You will not be sorry for making either investment; on the contrary, you will be grateful every day for the experience and opportunity to change your life for the better.

Power and strength…what you need to succeed.

> "Go around, under, over, and through until you get what you want."

SMACK: (Get your head in the game)

Go Green

Stop saying you don't like vegetables. Get that out of your head and get your head in the game of building a healthy, sexy body that rocks.

I always think back to the lessons I learned from my bodybuilding competition, when I realized the concepts of "can't" and "won't" had the biggest impact on my failures. I had ideas that I couldn't shake when I started the competition, I was wishy-washy at first, trying to talk myself into all the reasons that I couldn't do it instead of why I could. I asked my son Michael (25 and very wise) if he thought I could do it, given the obvious (to my warped way of thinking) obstacles I anticipated. His immediate response left me temporarily speechless: "Mom, if you think you can do it, you can do it. Stop talking about it and just do it." He didn't acknowledge or address that there were any obstacles. I taught my kids well but I hadn't instilled the lessons I taught them into my own life. I didn't remember that what we perceive becomes our reality. Our thoughts dictate if we can or can't. You always can. You are the only one standing in your own way. So step aside and let the magic happen.

You can try denying that self-worth, self-esteem, and self-confidence are tied to your weight and physical appearance, but you would be lying to yourself. Have you ever met someone who was overjoyed and buoyant because they were out of shape and overweight. Overweight goes hand in hand with feeling like crap, physically and emotionally. This extra weight is usually a cover-up, a protection, or a cry for help. It's not that you are your body. You are much, much more than that. However, you are housed in your body; and when you take good care of the place in which you live, everything else falls into place.

And here's where I get in trouble. People who preach that you should love your body no matter what shape it's in forget to tell you the rest of the story. You can and will start loving your body as it is today when you start taking extreme care of it today. If you are abusing yourself by overeating, binging, or eating toxic, inflammatory foods that you know are not good for you, then hours of affirmations and mantras of self-love will not work. Trying to manipulate thoughts in your head in order to create the illusion that you love your body is not going to work. You need to take the steps necessary to treat yourself well. Action steps that will inevitably change the outcome.

I figured it out and experienced my "aha moment". My conversion was as simple as switching on a light switch. And in an instant I knew that I would do it. All the naysayers came out of the woodwork, questioning my time, my commitment, my skill, my body, but I put the earplugs in and the blinders on and focused on what I would do, instead of what I couldn't do.

Yes, it was just that simple. I completely altered my thinking and the way I looked at the situation. I never doubted my commitment again, and I persevered, defying many statistical odds. I invested my heart and mind in my not so impossible feat, and I never looked back. If ever a negative thought popped into my head, it didn't stay long; I thanked it for sharing, dismissed it, and let it go, replacing it with what I knew I wanted.

If you take each day, each moment, each meal, and do the best you are capable of in that moment; choosing the healthiest options, you can be proud of yourself and begin to fall in love with the real you. You will know in your heart and soul that you are doing your very best, and no one can argue with that. Not even you.

Denying or making excuses for why you are not taking care of yourself won't get you anywhere but deeper into a slumpier slump with your food and the thinking processes (head games) that filter down to the rest of your body and the rest of your life. Are you getting the picture of how this is all connected?

Food, thoughts, love.

You can arrive at a place where you love and accept where you are, when you are participating fully in the process of treating yourself well. *If you are doing everything in your power and daily life to treat yourself with extreme care, valuing your body by making better food choices, making certain that you fuel yourself with whole, pure, real, and naked food, then yee-ha for you!* Make the spiritual connection between honoring yourself and your body and you will be at a place of peace, love, and acceptance of wherever you are. No matter what your weight or body type, you will be in love with it, and you will never care about a number on a scale.

Back to the Greens (and by the way, it is pretty easy to be green). Greens are in charge of cleaning up your body, providing nutrients, phytochemicals, and fiber to transport the junk right out of your system. They literally sweep the garbage out of you. Remember, it's easy to clean up your act by letting go of the food that is harming you and replacing that toxic food with better foods (mainly greens) that promote health and are delicious.

Think of your good eating habits as part of the 80/20 rule. Strive to make good naked choices 80 percent of the time (woo-hoo!), and 20 percent of the time you don't. It's what you do most of the time that counts, not what you do some of the time. Over indulging at one holiday meal does not need to unravel your new resolve. Recognize that you made some wise choices along with a smaller serving of whatever delicacy is calling your name and feel good about the abundance in your life, but then the next day make even more choices based on health than on cravings.

> *"Excessive weight attaches itself through persistent, consistent, overeating and bad choices."*

Similarly to the way poor quality, toxic food affects your health, body, and clear thinking, poor-quality, toxic people and relationships do the same. The challenge is to repeat the cleanup process for your relationships and other toxic situations that may be harming your health and well being.

Toxic humans may be relatives, co-workers or bosses, and that makes the cleanup process a bit more intense but you don't have to make it complicated or extreme. The cleanup may be as simple as reducing the amount of time spent with the person and/or creating a protective bubble around yourself at times when there is no option. Sit at the other end of the table and keep your close friends and family members nearby so you are protected and less affected by the poisons they produce.

Toxic food gives you a bellyache, indigestion, a sick feeling, or an overall feeling of "knowing you aren't eating right and taking good care of yourself"; toxic people will do the same. They can give you a real bellyache and a sick feeling every time you are with them. These bad guys leave you feeling apprehensive and nervous and sick to your stomach before, during, or after being in their presence. One visit every once in a while (20 percent) is similar to eating the popcorn and sugared gummy worms at the movie theater every once in a while. That 20 percent won't have the long-term ramifications that nightly indulgences of eating butter-soaked, salt-laden popcorn and sugared gummy worms every night would have.

Toxic people who are not physically in your life but who invade your mind are still jeopardizing your well being. Whenever I thought of the affects of toxic people, my ex-husband came to mind; I had to consistently work on the process of "letting go" to save myself. The resentment was highly poisonous to my body. Poison kills. That's it, in a nutshell. You don't want poison, even a little bit, anywhere near your precious presence. To free yourself from the poison, you gotta cut off the source. If you hold onto the poison, it will begin to infect other relationships too. Deciding to let go is cleansing, a cleaning out, a freedom, and it makes you feel awesome. Now when I think of my ex-husband, it is only with gratitude for the lessons I learned when I was with him. And that feeling is much more digestible and makes my tummy feel good instead of giving me indigestion. I choose to have a good feeling.

EXPERIENCE EXPERIMENT (Get your heart in the game)

Let It Go, Baby

It is an awesome experience to let go of our "woulda, coulda, shoulda's" and "counting, doubting, worrying", and that is what we will work on in this experience section.

Journaling is like no other experience. A pen in hand, releasing unfiltered thoughts through you, through your brain, through your body, flowing through your arm and down onto the paper—this is pure freedom.

There are scientific, energetic, and spiritual reasons why you feel instantly better when you engage in a letting-go experience, when you write stuff down, get it out of your head, and put it in a resting place outside yourself. You don't need to know how it works; you only need to know that it does work.

You turn on many light switches without thinking about why that switch works. I don't particularly know how a light switch works; I accept that it has something to do with Benjamin Franklin, a kite, a key, and an electrical storm, but beyond that I don't need to know why my electric switch turns the lights on and off or what's going on in the walls and wires. Con Ed has got my back. It's blind faith—I just believe.

I believe the lights will go on when I flip the switch, and they do. I am only interested in the result - light. Writing is electric. Don't question why writing, journaling, and letters of letting go work. Just trust that they do, and know that the result will be a "letting go" of negativity and a "bringing in" of contentment and liberation.

Get out your pen and paper, and let's get going. Let's let it go.

Toxic thoughts or resentment can eat away at you and short out your electricity. Identify one thought that you have that consistently picks away at your gut.

Be honest. Don't hold back.

Now is your chance to change and let the weight of toxic relationships slip off your shoulders.

Even if it is not always a strong or consistent feeling, you've got to let go. Imagine if every once in a while the kitchen lights just didn't switch on. You'd have to fix that, and right away too, because it would be annoying and dangerous to be walking around in the dark. Take a moment to think about the gut wrenching people or things that you are holding onto. Let's get rid of the toxin and get writing, dumping, letting go.

Take out a blank sheet of paper and a pen, and after considering your anguish, frustrations and resentments saturate the page or just jot down a simple statement of withdrawal. Write whatever thoughts of release are necessary. No one is going to read this letter except for you, so you are safe. Let it all out: clean up your gut, clear your mind, and set yourself free.

> *"Magic things happen when you put your thoughts on paper."*

You can burn this letter, rip up this letter, bury this letter. It's for your eyes only, so you should be as honest as you can be and allow all the poison to be released from your body and heart.

Fill it in. Let it go. All of it. Your letter to anyone about anything that is bugging you and weighing you down. Anything that you are just plain sick of holding onto that could be making you sick.

…Write on, baby.…Right on!

Here's an example of how you can start: Begin with "Dear.…" That's pretty easy, right?

Dear _____,

I let you go in love and peace. You no longer have control over me or affect me in any way. I release you and all negative _____.

SIGNED _____

LESSON 5

Lose the Fake Stuff And Get Real

Naked After 40 Vocabulary

Real deal:
Real food that is as close to its natural state as possible.

Pretty little boxes:
Deceptive packaging by food manufacturers that trick your eyes and stomach into believing they are "healthy".

Regular food store:
The typical American store filled with pretty little boxes.

Switch and ditch:
The knack of making better choices and healthier substitutions for the foods you love.

Real food does not come in pretty little boxes

Those pretty colorful boxes of food that are fancily placed at eye level throughout the grocery store have lots of not-so-healthy additives and ingredients that you may want to consider before you ingest them into that precious body of yours. They are fake food, made up in laboratories and factories to confuse your taste buds and wreak havoc on your beautiful body and destroy your health. Even small amounts of chemical ingredients are still poisonous. The standard American consumer who shops in a standard American grocery store is understandably in some serious trouble with health and weight. Perhaps it would not be so bad if once in a while, you eat a little of this or a little of that, but take what the average person eats regularly and the additives add up.

These lovely little boxes are just marketing gimmicks aimed directly at you and your family, containing misleading and dangerous messages that suck in trusting

Americans. It drives me crazy when I see false representation on boxes of so called food. Ever notice the check marks that suggest heart health is in the box? As a consumer, I guess it's natural to assume that what is written on the boxes is based in truth. But who is checking those misleading marketing messages? Many of them are not even based on legitimate nutritional research.

So what's the point of a label when you can't do the math without having three college degrees and a magic ball to help predict the hidden or disguised ingredients?

When they print "100% whole grains" on a bread label, what do they really mean? If you think "100 % whole grain bread", you'd be wrong! Here's how it goes…. If the first ingredient in your bread contains the word "whole", it is likely but not guaranteed that the product is whole grain. If the word "grains" is first on the label, but only the second ingredient has the word "whole", it can contain as little as 1% whole grain or as much as 49%. Now I say that is not only confusing but misleading as well. But it gets even worse. Suppose you said "WOO HOO, I am eating "multi grain" bread!" because that's what you read on the package. But the ingredient list on the package also includes "enriched white flour, whole wheat flour, whole oat flour"…, you still can't be sure from the label whether the product is made up of 70% whole grains or 7%.

Enter the Whole Grains Council (WGC).

According to its website (www.wholegrainscouncil.org), the WGC "is a nonprofit consumer advocacy group working to increase consumption of whole grains for better health." This group developed product packaging stamps for "easier" comprehension but as far as I can read, they are even more confusing unless you're willing to go into the website and do some extra research (and while you're there check out the founders of the group, you'll see some easily recognizable companies.) The group put the stamps on packaging to remind you to eat 48g of whole grains each day. And for those of you who are not going to the website – here's my understanding. They make two labels, one (the Basic Stamp) indicates some of the grain is whole grain but the product may include refined flour as well. The other is the 100% stamp promising that "ALL of the grain (in the product) is whole grain". Up until 2006 the WGC had three stamps that suggested good sources, excellent sources and 100 % excellent sources of whole grains. So if you get a package with one of those labels…it's old and confusing. The WGC states that you can eat 3 grain food products labeled 100 % or 6 products with any whole grains for example. Does that mean that I can eat 6 slices of not so nutritious bread? I don't know about you but I confused myself writing this section.

When you start checking out the fat content on a label, it gets even worse because there is no National Fat Council to put a stamp on your food to help you decipher it. And you may be thinking fat is bad from years of being told that big fat lie. Food labels declaring "low fat" mean an item contains 3g of fat or less, or 30% or less of total calories. Reduced fat means it contains 25 % or less. Lite foods mean 50% or less than in comparable foods. So do they expect when you are shopping that you will have a handy dandy chart with you for deciphering the percentages?

Before I became "aware", I shopped in a "regular" grocery store with my coupons and bought what was on sale without concern. I trusted that the store and the manufacturer knew what was good for me. I never thought they would be lying to me or intentionally trying to confuse me. Hey we're talking about a person's health here! How dare they!

Remember the Seinfeld episode when they were all eating the advertised "FAT FREE" ice cream and they were all getting fat? That's kind of the way American grocery stores are betraying our waist lines as Americans grow fatter and unhealthier every day all the while devouring every new box of "lite", "reduced fat" and "fat free" chemical-laden, processed food we find displayed seductively on the shelf.

I think I have made the point quite clear. You need to make the effort to "Know what the frig' you are eating".

> *"Become the advocate for your health, become a food detective, a guard, and a protector of your own body"*

It is your body, you are in control, and you have the choice and the power to protect it. It is both your right and your obligation to treat yourself well.

Who will benefit if you don't take care of yourself?

_____
_____
_____

Who will benefit if you do take care of yourself?

___

___

Who have you been trusting with your health?

___

___

Hey, you there, dutifully looking at that rectangle of "nutritional facts" on that box? You're on the wrong side!

Get on the right side—the side of the box that tells you the truth.

For years and years, in my prior days of food ignorance, deprivation, and boxed diets—in my store/manufacturer-trusting days—I would read and obsess over the calorie, fat, carbohydrate, and sugar content of everything I bought. That changed as I discovered the part that I was missing.

NUTRITION TRANSITION (Get your body in the game)

Think Outside the Box

What I learned, and what I share with you now is a simple philosophy on food choice. I will show you how to make intelligent decisions regarding what you put into your body without having a doctorate in nutrition, a text book or handy, dandy calculator. Who needs all that? You're so busy, do you really need to make such a big deal and stress out about your food choices. I say NO way! I want to make sure that when you shop, you are armed and protected with simple knowledge that can keep you healthy. You gotta look at the correct side of the box. You've been focused on the wrong side. Switch sides—realize that looking at calories is not getting you anywhere. The gold lies in the ingredients list. It shows you immediately if this is a product that you should put into your one and only very precious body.

One company, who purports to be REAL, really pissed me off with their boxes of ice pops labeled "Fruit Bars," that states clearly on the front of the box "made with real fruit," and then, as I went on to read the ingredients to check for the so-called real fruit, I read the following:

"Water, sugar, lime juice from concentrate, citric acid, lime pulp, natural flavors, guar gum, carob bean gum, lime and lemon peel, yellow #5, and green #3."

Did I miss something here? Like the REAL FRUIT? Like, really?

Now this is annoying to me, because to me, it's blatant misrepresentation. A bold-faced lie, in writing. Seriously, is lemon and lime peel considered real fruit? This type of thing gives you one more job to do; because now it is up to you to discover and know for yourself what the frig' you are eating.

This is also what I call reading the "right" side of the box - the side with the ingredients list. This very important side of the box is where the ingredients are listed; this is where you will find all the information that matters.

This is the recipe I shared in chapter one (I hope you have tried it already.) These bars are yummy delish and easy to make with the simplest of ingredients. They are as pure and naked as you can get. (You can get more recipes like this on www.cookingnakedafter40.com, where I personally test and approve of every single recipe before I share it.)

If we were looking at the ingredient side of the box (i.e. my recipe), the ingredient list of "Rosie's Pure and Naked "Apple Oat Bars" is:

1. bananas
2. apples
3. walnuts
4. raisins
5. pumpkin
6. coconut
7. oatmeal

Let's compare those ingredients with the ingredients on the side of a box of "a famously nationally recognized brand," Oatmeal to Go Bars (clearly marked with a check mark symbol suggesting and guaranteeing that you are making a "Smart Choice"; the label on the box says, "smart choices made easy"). My first question would be to ask what they mean when they say "Natural & Artificial Flavors"? That's right on the front of the box in bold letters, so you can't miss it. My question, again, is why would you put anything artificial in your precious body? Cut down your shopping time; if you see "artificial" anything" plainly printed on the front of the box, you don't have to waste your time reading any other information. Put it down and move on.

"Artificial" anything is a no-no, so just by simply seeing that word, you have all you need to know. It's a "no" for this product.

For me, I go by the rule that this real woman (me) eats nothing artificial! I mean really, why would I? Why would you?

For the sake of the learning experience, if we choose to ignore the artificial notification on the front and go to the ingredients list, it reads like this. My comments are italicized, starred and bolded. Sorry, but I just could not help myself from commenting. I want to scream (can you hear me?), but instead I just added comments. The rest of the stuff really is listed on the box of bars. I couldn't make this up if I tried.

1. whole grain rolled oats
2. high fructose corn syrup *sugar*
3. oat bran concentrate
4. brown sugar more *sugar*
5. sugar *we need more sugar?*
6. oat flour
7. dried apples (treated with sulfur dioxide to promote color retention)
8. margarine (partially hydrogenated soybean oil, soybean oil, water, partially hydrogenated cottonseed oil, salt, mono- and diglycerides, soy lecithin, calcium disodium EDTA (a preservative), annatto color, artificial flavor, vitamin A palmitate)
9. maltodextrin
10. glycerin
11. modified food starch
12. corn syrup *a little more sugar*
13. rice flour
14. dried whole eggs
15. malted barley extract
16. calcium carbonate
17. water
18. salt
19. cinnamon
20. natural and artificial flavors *what do you mean, and why don't you have to tell me what they are?*
21. sorbitol *a little more sweetness, just in case*
22. corn cereal *I thought this was oatmeal*
23. partially hydrogenated cottonseed and/or soybean oil
24. wheat flour

25. sodium bicarbonate
26. corn flour
27. malic acid
28. malt (contains barley, soy, wheat components)
29. sodium alginate *sounds like fish tank droppings*
30. enzyme modified soy protein
31. turmeric color
32. natural mixed tocopherols
33. yellow 6 *I prefer to wear my yellow color on my shoes rather than eat it*
34. calcium phosphate
35. sodium hexametaphosphate *hope I spelled this correctly—I certainly can't pronounce it*
36. artificial color *that's not fair, why aren't you sharing the colors with us? What color is an oatmeal bar supposed to be, anyhow?*
37. niacinamide *sounds like something James Bond would have to use in an emergency*
38. vitamin A palmitate
39. potassium sorbate and BHT *preservatives*
40. reduced iron *are they taking iron out?*
41. sodium phosphate
42. pyridoxine hydrochloride *sounds armed and dangerous to me*
43. riboflavin
44. thiamin mononitrate
45. folic acid *you can get this from your veggies*

*Did I make my point clearly?

Forty-five ingredients? And that's not including the individual crap that "might be"? in the margarine. WTF? What would your body do with all of those extra preservatives, anyway?

For whom would you make this recipe that includes 45 ingredients in its attempt to create a product that needs fewer than 7 whole ingredients?

Which list of ingredients would make your body grateful - my recipe or the store-bought kind?

Now you have an easy shopping trick. You don't need to have a nutrition degree, be a scientist, or have a calculator. You just need to read, and if you can't read or pronounce what's in it, don't buy it. If there are more than five or six ingredients, you may want to consider trying a different brand or item. Different brands offer different versions of the same food. You don't have to give up what you like, just buy better so you can eat better so you can feel better.

> *"Buy better so that you can eat better so that you can feel better. We can have a say in what our stores stock. Talk to the manager about the products you'd like to see and talk with your money. If we stop buying these unhealthy products, food manufacturers will stop producing them."*

Now that you are armed with knowledge and information, use your power wisely. Monitor what goes into your shopping cart and especially into that precious body of yours. Your body has got a lot to do in this life. It needs and wants to be healthy, because it has the job of getting you around in fine fashion. For that to happen, you've got to participate in keeping it healthy and well. You are in total control of what goes into it.

Remember the only thing between the fork that you hold in your hand and your mouth and the food you put in it, is your head (and of course the excuses you create).

> *"Think outside the box: if you are reading a lot of labels, you are eating too much processed food."*

It is not complicated to eat naked. No label is a good label. The fewer ingredients, the healthier the food.

Remember, the following foods have no label. They're direct from nature and God (start thinking this way...add to the list the naked foods you love). Think simple, green, clean, pure, no label, naked.

- green apples
- pears
- bananas
- sweet potatoes
- green kale
- apricots
- kiwi
- nuts—almonds, walnuts, cashews
- seeds
- quinoa
- brown rice
- coconut

If you are thinking, "OMG, this is so much work", your thinking is out of alignment. Lose that old story. We are creatures of habit, and we eat most of the same foods most of time anyway. Once you select a brand you like that is pure and naked, stick with it. I love "Crazy Richard's Natural Peanut Butter." It lists only peanuts on its label. Why do I like it? Maybe because the label is bright pink but also because I like the creamy consistency, and once you stir it, it stays that way even in the refrigerator. I don't need to experiment or read every peanut butter jar when I go grocery shopping. I just purchase the one that I know fills my need, tastes good, and is good for me.

People are heavier than ever and sicker than ever in our country. Sure, we might be living longer—but we are living longer on medications. Most Americans are taking some form of medication to control some dysfunction in their bodies. Most of these would be correctable by adjusting food consumption.

Conduct your own experiment. When you are chatting with friends, make a mental note of how many people are "on drugs" and the number of pharmaceuticals they are taking for all kinds of reasons that could be prevented and solved by a change in diet. I am not a doctor, nor do I try to be, nor do I suggest you get off any meds that you are on, for major changes in lifestyle consult with your doctor. But I do suggest that you read your labels and remember the simple rules:

- The fewer ingredients the better.

- If you can't pronounce it, don't eat it.
- If your great grandma didn't use it for her food, don't use it for yours.
- Be a food detective and monitor what goes into your body.

SMACK: (Get your head in the game)

Ditch and Switch

Do a ditch and switch (sounds like a dance move and maybe you just might be dancing more when your body is feeling better). I provided a list of foods you can ditch and offered you a better option to switch to. I've done the research and discovered great brands to suggest for your switch that will be healthier than what you are currently using.

As we are in the SMACK (Baditude Adjustment) section of this lesson, we will also be addressing the old mindset about eating healthy that may not be working for you. You may start now to ditch your current way of thinking about food and switch to a better mindset. Get your head and new way of thinking in the game of weight loss and self esteem.

I was shocked during a food assessment with a client that her biggest fear was that she would have to give up enjoyment and pleasure around food. She was so resistant to changing and eating healthier, because she had the idea that "healthy food is boring" and suggested she would rather stay unhealthy than give up the fun. I was slightly insulted and asked her point blank: "Do you think that I don't have fun in my life?" I explained to her that I loved my food and that healthy food doesn't mean boring food. You can love what you eat. I eat often. I eat a lot. I eat yum-azing food. I love what I eat. You will, too."

Clients tell me that they love the new way of cooking, eating, tasting, and the easy recipes.

One woman who had been cooking and eating naked for the last six months was shocked to discover that as she lightened up about her food and gave herself permission to have cake if she wanted it, she actually chose not to have it…she really didn't want it. After eating amazing food, your body doesn't crave the junk. She also shared her experience the night she went on a candy binge and was very sick the next day, loopy, out of sorts, and not able to function as normal. How scary is it to realize that she had grown so accustomed to bad crap in her foods that until she "detoxed" she wasn't aware or able to hear her body tell her it wanted better treatment and food. She told me that it was a great experiment, and she was no longer willing to give up a day in her life by feeling physically and mentally ill from a sugar rush. She told me, "It is not worth it—at all!" You can experience this too—and you will.

Knowing that you can still have what you want (but in a healthier way) will get you to relax, open up to new ideas, and commit to trying new things. Be patient. It may take you some time, and that's okay. It's a creative form of concocting and cooking. Once you experience and practice a few recipes, you will become an expert with your own creations. You will enjoy it, because you'll be eating fabulous, delicious flavors in new and creative ways. In my recipes, I combine pure, naked foods in a multitude of ways so they always excite the senses, enhance the plate and delight the palette.

When you are ditching and switching, remember to read the ingredients list and pick the brand with the fewest and purest. Here are a few quick switches to get you started.

DITCH	SWITCH
JIF Peanut Butter - contains roasted peanuts, fully hydrogenated vegetable oil, mono- and diglycerides, molasses, sugar, and salt	**Crazy Richard's Natural Peanut Butter** contains peanuts
Activia Yogurt (blueberry flavor) reduced-fat milk, sugar, fructose, strawberries, blueberry puree, water, modified food starch, natural flavor, kosher gelatin, agar agar, lactic acid, carrageenan, calcium lactate, sodium citrate, xanthan gum, vitamin D 3	**Fage Greek Yogurt** Grade A pasteurized skim milk, live active yogurt cultures (L. Bulgaricus, S. Thermophilus, L. Acidophilius, Bifidus, Casei)

DITCH	SWITCH
Kellogg's Special K - contains wheat gluten, sugar, defatted wheat germ, salt, high fructose corn syrup, dried whey, malt flavorings, calcium caseinate, ascorbic acid, alpha tocopherol acetate, reduced iron, pyridoxine hydrochloride, riboflavin, thiamine hydrochloride, palmitate, folic acid, vitamin B12	Cream of Rice Cereal brown rice
Welch's Grape Jelly - concord grapes, corn syrup, high fructose corn syrup, fruit pectin, citric acid, sodium citrate	St. Dalfour Strawberry Preserves strawberries, concentrated grape juice, fruit pectin, lemon juice
Pepperidge Farm Whole Grain Farmhouse Bread - wheat flour whole, wheat flour, unbromated unbleached enriched flour, barley malted flour, niacin, iron reduced thiamine mononitrate, Vitamin B1, B2, folic acid, corn syrup, high fructose, oat fiber, yeast, wheat gluten, soybean oil, butter, nonfat milk, honey, salt, calcium sulfate, sugar, calcium propionate, datem, mono- and diglycerides, soy lecithin, enzymes, folic acid	Food for Life EZEKIEL Bread organic sprouted wheat, filtered water, organic raisins, organic sprouted barley, organic sprouted millet, organic sprouted lentils, organic sprouted soybeans, or sprouted spelt, fresh yeast, organic wheat gluten, sea salt, organic cinnamon
Start your own journey here by taking the information you just learned along with your newly prescribed reading glasses and go shopping.	

You will see the difference of what's in the product by looking at the ingredients list, but the best part is that your body will feel the difference when you eat the product with fewest ingredients and fewest refined, refurbished, and processed stuff.

Make more switches for your health. Transition to whole, pure, and naked eating without frustration or sacrificing the tastes and experiences that you currently love. Give your taste buds a chance to change, and you'll be loving your new food, feeling better, and looking "gorgeous-er" in no time.

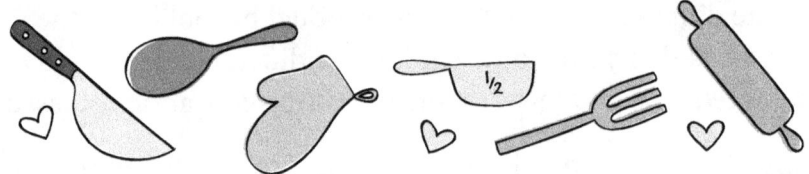

YUM. NAKED RECIPE:

TRY PB&J THE "NAKED" WAY.

- 2 slices cinnamon raisin Ezekiel bread
- 1 TBSP Crazy Richard's peanut butter
- 1 tsp St. Dalfour strawberry jam
- 1/2 sliced banana
- 1 TBSP coconut oil

Melt a dab of virgin coconut oil in a pan and heat pan. When the pan is hot, place sandwich in it and brown both sides. The peanut butter will melt, the bread will toast, and you'll be in peanut butter heaven.

EXPERIENCE EXPERIMENT (Get your heart in the game)

Kitchen Cabinet Pitch

Let's focus on three things you can do to clean up your cabinets. But in order to really throw CRAP out, you've got to first fall in love with the idea and get your heart into this game. You can't be feeling guilty about it. You may have to lose the idea that you are WASTING FOOD when you are cleaning your cabinets and purging the garbage food. Just keep focused on the fact that garbage belongs in the trash and politely place those junk filled, processed foods into that trash can.

> *"Garbage (food) belongs in the trash, not in your healthy, sexy body."*

List the crap you are pitching and why you are pitching it. This little exercise will help with your justification and guilt:

_____

_____

SALAD DRESSING

What brand are you currently using?

_____

_____

What are the ingredients? List them here. Do I need extra lines? Now ask yourself: Are they simple, pure, and naked enough for my precious, healthy, sexy body?

_____

_____

What kind of dressing will you choose now? (with your new ditch and switch skills, you can shop around, if you still want to buy prepared dressings.) List the ingredients in your new choice. What is better about this new choice?

_____

_____

When you are ready, you have the option of trying the "naked dressing recipe" in Chapter Four, so you can begin to make your own dressings. Check out my videos on www.cookingnakedafter40.com if you would like to see how easy it is to prepare a healthy, pure, and naked dressings.

PEANUT BUTTER

What are you currently using?

_____

_____

Look for added palm oils, hydrogenated oils, and salt. Peanut butter should be just that: peanuts only!

What are the ingredients on your jar? List them here. Are they simple, pure, and naked enough for your precious, healthy, sexy body?

_____

_____

What will you switch it to? Why? What is better about this new choice?

_____

_____

Tip: try almond butter or cashew butter for a change. Double yum.

List the ingredients in your new choice:

_____

_____

_____

COLD CEREAL

What are you currently using?

_____

_____

What are the ingredients? List them here. Are they simple, pure, and naked enough for your precious, healthy, sexy body?

_____

_____

Why are you ditching what you are currently using?

_____

_____

What will you switch it to? Why?

_____

_____

List the ingredients in your new choice:

_____

_____

_____

Start slowly. Don't overwhelm yourself. The results show up in huge ways from the small changes that you make. Keep going. Make it fun. Fall in love with getting healthy. Become a food detective and a protector of your body.

List 3 changes that you will implement in your life after reading this lesson:

1. _____
2. _____
3. _____

It's reward time for accomplishing another chapter. Pick up a bouquet of fresh flowers from the grocery store when you go shopping. They will brighten your day.

LESSON 6

Falling In Love With Yourself

Naked After 40 Vocabulary

Fatheadedness:
Constantly thinking fat thoughts about yourself.

Extraordinary:
The result of falling in love with everything you do

Pant chants:
The "I can't fit in my pants" syndrome that causes lack of self-esteem, decreased confidence, and often depression.

You are unique and gorgeous!

You have beauty deep down. Sometimes that inner beauty gets hidden and squashed because you are not loving yourself enough to take good care of yourself. If your unique brilliance is hidden inside an unhealthy physical body, you are stuck and are not fully healthy and happy. You can change that. You can fall in love with you.

Doesn't sound so easy? Where do you start? You start by "falling in love with the idea". The idea is building your version of your healthiest sexiest self.

Love and abuse are opposites. You can't do one when you are doing the other. Therefore beating yourself up for not being perfect is not going to be an option when you are in love. Get it? The self abuse and negative thinking about yourself are bad habits you developed over time. At some point during your childhood, you locked onto an image of yourself based on what you learned, saw, and experienced that suggested you needed to act and look a certain way. Now, when you don't live up to this ridiculously old, ineffective and worn out concept of perfection, you lose sight of self-love and end up with the opposite feeling. Know what I'm talking about?

I want to share a conversation that I recently had with an acquaintance—a forty-eight-year-old, beautiful woman, who went on and on about how bad she looked because she was a size 6 now, and there were some size 4's and even some size 2's in her closet.

I had no idea what she was talking about by looking at her. She looked perfect and beautiful to me. But she had it in her head that she was fat, and it was holding her back. She was what I refer to as a "fathead", constantly thinking fat thoughts about herself and acting fat. If she had talked about me the way she was talking about herself, I would never talk to her again. She went on and on about how she fit into the smaller size last year and was really angry at herself for letting "this" happen.

So let's sum up her whole obsessive problem - Her pants didn't fit.

After listening to her go on and on about this, I simply said, "Perhaps you need to buy new pants that come with a new healthy, sexy mindset.

NUTRITION TRANSITION (Get your body in the game)

Body Kindness

Do you wake up every morning disappointed, scared and dreading the grueling task of getting dressed. Grueling because nothing fits and your clothes are tight.

Like my friend who needed a new pair of pants, regardless of whether you are carrying around an additional five, ten, fifteen, thirty, or forty plus pounds, your head is affected and your attitude follows suit for the day.

If your weight or your fatheadedness is holding you back from "your greatness" and the possibility of "big" things you can do, then it is time to do something about it.

> *"If feeling "big" in your body is making you play it "small" in your business or life, then you've got to do something right now."*

You have a choice. You can stay that way and fully accept it. Throw out those pants that don't fit and buy new ones. Or you can do what it takes to make the changes to get the results that you want.

So what do you really want?

How much could you accomplish, and how much more would you do, if you felt amazing and were truly comfortable in your body? What would it be like if you had all the time and energy and brain space you currently devote to dieting to use in more productive, loving and fun ways? What words could you use to describe how that would feel?

_____

_____

What would you need to change right now to feel comfortable in your body?

_____
_____
_____

Living in your ideal body begins with self-love, not with restrictive dieting. Once you start to treat yourself and your body well, you can fully accept yourself and your body as it is right now while loving yourself fully as the changes are happening. This is what I call "falling in love with the idea." Falling in love with the process of growing healthier and sexier makes the journey much more palatable and very delicious. In this particular area, we'll call it "Body Kindness". Body Kindness is approaching each meal as the opportunity to grow healthier and sexier and the perfect opportunity to practice kindness to your body. You can start the process right now, right this moment, and you don't have to wait until Monday morning. Self-love begins in this moment, this very moment. No matter what day it is, begin now.

Love yourself enough to take extreme care of yourself. This doesn't mean restricting calories or dieting (and then un-dieting). It's actually not very nice to treat yourself in such a harsh way. Self care and body kindness means taking each meal and making it the best and healthiest meal it can be at that moment, in that situation. You can do that. It's simply focusing on only one meal at a time. Do you ever find yourself making bad choices at a meal because in your head you justify that you can start the new process and eat healthy at the next meal? When you switch that thinking that you can start tomorrow to knowing that you have the opportunity in front of you to start right now, everything changes.

The best you can do at every moment is personal, it's the best YOU can do at every moment. Changing your mind will change your body. Your body would thank you for loving yourself enough, for doing your very best by responding with health, feeling good, performing better, and showing up gorgeously. You would exude a healthy, radiant beauty and glow from every pore. People will ask you, "What are you doing to look so radiant, glowing and gorgeous"?

Think of your children (if you are a mom) or someone you love more than anything, and it will help you to understand this philosophy. You would never consider knowingly feeding your beloved even one meal that would not be good for them. Every meal counts. You wouldn't accept it if they were abusing their bodies by being unkind, overeating or eating food that would hurt them. (yes I am saying that processed food will hurt you over time as you invite diseases that are fueled by years of poor eating) You love them so much that you want the best for them and for their lives. So when it comes to yourself, why would you accept anything less?

> "Self-love is not a selfish act. It is actually the most generous gift you can give to the world. Presenting your best self to the world means you are performing at optimal levels, and you will be the best mom, best wife, best employee/employer, best friend you can be".

What fatheaded thoughts are coming into your mind right now?
_____
_____
_____

If your body was healthy and fit and you were at your "ideal" weight, how would your internal thoughts be different?
_____
_____
_____

What more would you do in your life or be willing to try if you felt healthier and sexier? Would relationships change? Would job opportunities change?
_____
_____
_____

What could you accomplish that you aren't even attempting right now?
_____
_____
_____

What could you do differently in a healthier body with a healthier mindset?
_____
_____

What would change in your life? How would it be different?
_____
_____
_____

How would showing up in a physically "different" body affect the way you participate in your life?
_____
_____
_____

Here is an opportunity to make a small change right now by implementing one small tip that will make a big difference. It's "the little idea", "the big push", "the secret weapon", "the magic pill", "the shifter", "the whatever it takes", "the whatever-you-call-it" thing that will ignite the process of change and incite the magic to happen.

Are you ready to try something different?
Are you ready to try something new?
How about a meat-free Monday,
That is really yummy, too.

Let's make a shift now - a simple change, a do-able change, a fun change. This is something you have control of, a physical act that you can experience. Let's rename your Monday. Instead of your old pattern of using Monday as the new day to start a diet, let's rename it Meat-Free Monday and use it as a day to make a positive change in the way you eat. The concept of Meat-Free Monday is to try a new way of eating by incorporating and concocting a new meat-free meal. Trying something different produces different results. This small, once a week change is not really extreme but it will produce extraordinary results.

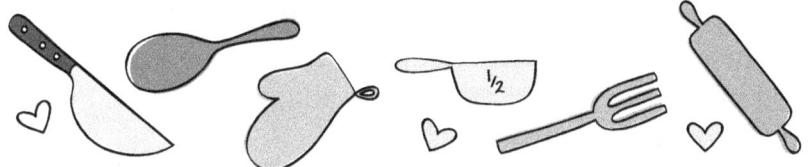

YUM. NAKED RECIPE:

"MEAT" (free) LOAF (minus the meat—shh!—no one will ever know)

- 1/2 cup raw cashews
- 1/2 cup raw pecans
- 1 cup raw walnuts
- 1 red bell pepper
- 1 medium ripe tomato
- 1/2 cup minced onion
- 1/2 cup chopped celery
- 3 cloves minced garlic
- 2 TBSP fresh cilantro
- salt and pepper to taste (or any other spices)

Put all ingredients in a food processor and pulse until mixed, but not pureed. Take mixture and form into the shape of a loaf; put on a pretty platter. There's no sweating over a hot stove, no burning yourself while cooking naked. You do not have to heat this "meat"free loaf (although you can heat it if you want to). Just throw it together and enjoy.

Serve with up with some

AVOCADO-TOMATO CREAM:
- 1 avocado
- 1 large tomato
- 1 lime, juice squeezed out
- Salt and pepper
- handful of cilantro

Blend together until creamy using a Vitamix or high powered blender. This is a creamy, delicious topping for the meat-free loaf or a dressing to complement your green salad.

Of course, using a beautiful plate to present your new amazingly naked and nutritious, healthy, sexy meat-free loaf changes the meal even more. You are improving the quality of how you eat visually, instead of slapping something down on a paper plate. We'll save the slapping for the Smack section.

This is how you change one meal at a time - one moment at a time. Enjoy the experience of creating this great new dish and the opportunity to invent and reinvent every meal and make it exciting.

Allow the process to unfold and celebrate by making Monday a day of experimentation. This will help unglue the old behaviors that were stuck in your mind and give you some new kitchen adventures. Meat-free Monday recipes are a great way for you to start making changes with small steps that are implementable and sustainable.

Not available on Mondays? No worries.

I've got that excuse covered. It doesn't have to be Monday; use your imagination and pick a day of the week that works for you,. Give yourself the opportunity, freedom and permission to do something different and fun. Remember: "less" (meat) means "more" (health).

Need more ideas for small changes that could be fun?

How about a "Salad Sunday"? (Make it an all green day!)

"Try something new on Tuesdays"? Or designate it as "Naked Tuesday" (and get "naked" every Tuesday with a new naked recipe experiment).

How about a "Smoothie Saturday," where you drink decadently delicious smoothies for the day?

This is exciting and fun, not complicated or difficult. You can't screw up, because, you are the creator and you make up the rules. This is how you fall in love with the idea of health.

SMACK: (Get your head in the game)

Xtreme to Xtraordinary

Extreme care doesn't mean you have to be extreme in what you do. It means you have to be extraordinary.

Extraordinary means doing everything you do with a little extra oomph—or, better said, with LOVE! Extraordinary means falling in love with everything you do—even the mundane tasks like taking out the trash. It means being the best "trash taker-outer" you can be. Put a smile on your face and know that you are the best you can be in every moment of your extraordinary life.

The little extras are just that, "little". These are not big changes; they are small easily adoptable changes that yield big results.

I invite you to brainstorm about little extras (nothing extreme) you could add to your daily life, that would make an extraordinary difference in how you look and feel.

Complete the exercise below, because the experience and awareness of how this concept works will carry over into everything you do. It will help you feel less overwhelmed as you break down the bigger picture of the huge project looming in front of you. It will keep you from giving up or getting stuck and feeling overwhelmed.

I want to share my closet story as an example. I admit it: I am a clothes hound. I love clothes. My closet is oversized. Actually, it's a whole bedroom, and recently I was presented with the overwhelming task of organizing what I had let get out of control. It could take hours or days to go through, purge, and reorganize.

I could set up that big day devoted completely to my closet and probably never get the full chunk of time necessary to complete the task. The very thought seemed so daunting that it set me up to create the excuses I needed to never find the time to get it done. In my head, it was a huge mountainous task. Add to that the fact that I could still find things, and the issue wasn't an emergency. I didn't have a whole day to put aside. This is a fine example of something that was not painful enough to motivate me immediately. It sat on a list of things I wanted to change but chose to tolerate instead. Tolerating things that annoy you is heavy and "weighty".

What are some things you may be tolerating right now? (people, places, things)
_____
_____
_____

How are these tolerances affecting how you feel?

How are they weighing you down, physically, emotionally, spiritually?
_____
_____
_____

Taking something off your tolerance list is like taking weight off your shoulders. I decided to change my approach on this project, as my original plan of a one day attack never seemed to manifest and my tolerance grew heavier and heavier. Days, months, and seasons came and went with my messy closet a constant and disappointing reminder of what I could not get accomplished. It weighed on my mind and body.

So, I did something. And here is what I did differently…

I was less extreme but more extraordinary.

1. I decided to fall in love with the idea of how it would feel every day to have a clean, organized, walk-in closet to start my day. I really wanted the feeling that my clean closet promised: light, easy, beautiful.

2. I became aware that having an organized, beautiful closet would be an example of extreme care of myself. That is important to me, and so tolerating it any other way was just not good enough anymore.

3. Displaying my beautiful clothes with care makes me happy, so I made the choice that that was what I wanted.

4. I created a plan of action, focusing on one small step. I designated one small chunk

of time every day for a week, and the results accumulated. The small changes yielded the big result in the end. My closet was clean.

By handling it this way, I didn't feel overwhelmed by the burden of getting it all done at once. I knew that all the little steps would add up, with the end result being what I wanted. Do you see the correlation to your health and weight-loss efforts?

Whatever project you choose to get accomplished, use this as an example. If something needs adjusting and is pinging you, pushing you, annoying you, you need to create the extraordinary or I call it "X" factor. Doing that little eXtra thing each day will provide eXtraordinary results. As for my closet story, it simply meant that I would spend fifteen to twenty minutes a day, organizing. (Take out your handy dandy timer and set it for your 15 minutes of action - when it rings you can move on or continue but you are now in control of a previously out of control situation) I organized my stocking drawer, then my blouses, then my sweaters, and on and on until my intention was realized. The result was a closet that I love to walk into with easy-to-find items, my clothes all cared for respectfully; a pleasurable experience for me every morning when I get dressed. This is an example of how little extra things have an extraordinary effect on your life and your feelings. I have replaced my mess with beauty, and that makes me feel lighter, leaner, cared for, and beautiful.

Apply this principle to everything you do, and you'll see your world transform before your very eyes.

What project is looming large before you, weighing you down? (FYI this heavy project or thought can actually be putting and keeping extra physical weight on you.)

_____

_____

What can you choose to do that will allow you to get this project off your overloaded plate of life?

_____

_____

EXPERIENCE EXPERIMENT (Get your heart in the game)

How I Love Thee

Are you your own biggest critic, toughest judge, and perhaps worst enemy? When you start picking on yourself and your body parts, are you brutal?

My daughter, who is an amazing athlete and basketball player, strong and beautiful, was complaining that her thighs were too big. Now, I can assure you that if you looked at these twenty-one-year-old thighs, you would want them for your own, and you'd think she was nuts, for sure. Her internal judge and critic decided that they were too big.

We discussed this in detail one day and came to the conclusion that if she did not have bigger, stronger thighs, she may not be the successful college athlete that she is. Her very "pinging" body part is actually her strength. With time and a bit of support—prompted by me and practiced by her—she was able to accept and see the beauty of her thighs. She decided she would write a letter to her thighs and thank them for all the beautiful things they do for her, for the beautiful way they support her and help her run and jump high and fast in her collegiate basketball games.

Here is your opportunity to get naked with yourself.

What is the one area of your body that you pick on the most?

_____

_____

What sorts of daily complaints do you make to that body part?

_____

How can you switch it, think differently like my daughter did, and how can you instead find the love that your body part needs and deserves?

What will you say now, with your new frame of reference? What will you thank this picked-on part for?

I am borrowing my daughter's idea and suggesting that you create your own "loving letter" to your body. Okay, it may sound weird, but it will help you focus your energies and come up with a specific plan of action to alter your mindset. I'll help you along with some until you get this rolling along on your own.

DEAREST BODY OF MINE,

Specifically speaking to my _____ name your body part),

You are... _____

I used to think... _____

I now see differently, and I see in you... _____

I now know that you are... _____

I love you for... _____

I need you for... _____

I appreciate you for... _____

(for example, you could say things like:

You are...a magnificent piece of machinery.

I used think ...that you, my thighs, were too fat for my body.

I now know that you are...strong and beautiful)

I thank you for... _____

I love and appreciate your... _____

I will stop calling you... _____

and start referring to you in more loving terms like... _____

With all my love, gratitude, and appreciation for doing the job perfectly,

Signed,

xxooxx

List 3 changes that you will implement in your life after reading this lesson:

1. _____
2. _____
3. _____

Pick up a bouquet of flowers today in honor of your accomplishments and the changes you are implementing

LESSON 7

Are We There Yet?

Naked After 40 Vocabulary

Fat chance:
The opportunity to relearn the facts about healthy fats.

Practice and repeat:
The development of negative self-talk.

Bars and jars:
The learned language of self-abuse; consisting of words such as "I cheated," "I was bad," "I am so mad at myself," or "I can't lose weight no matter what I do."

Are we there yet?

This may be the most frequently asked question by kids in cars. It's also an adult question. We're wired for a "goal", a "get", or a "want" and we may desire a certain place or thing that will prove to us that we've arrived. But is there ever a "there"? Since life is changing constantly every single day, how can there be a "there"? And even if there were, how long would it be there before it changed again? Even more importantly, what will you do when you get there?

If you enjoyed your day today. I mean really enjoyed your day and made it special, wouldn't those individual days add up to a life filled with special days. If you do the math that would add up to a very enjoyable extraordinary life, just because you made every day the best it could be. Actively participating in the moment changes everything. It sounds so easy but those little insidious misery mongers send the "fear" and "doubt" thoughts right into your brain and then you snap right out of the moment.

How many times do you remember being consumed by worry about something that "might" happen sometime in the distant future? You could be doing that right now. Most of the time, however, the very things we waste our time and energy "worrying" about and stressing over, never even happen at all.

I had a client who needed to lose one hundred pounds. After week one of working with me and cooking "naked," she had lost five pounds. She was upset and said, "I wish it could be faster." My reply, "Patience and gratitude, please."

We had an unanticipated snowstorm in October one year that wreaked some havoc on my neighborhood, knocking out electrical power for 6 days. Since it was only October, the weather was turning nippy but not nasty; however, I was nasty. The loss of power affected my attitude, and I became a complaining, cold, and whiny woman. I wanted my lights and my heat. I complained so much that I missed the gold in the week. You may be saying what gold could there have been in a week of chaos where everything was slightly off and out of whack? The gold was in front of me. Because I had no lights at night, I was invited to a dear friends home to sit by the fireplace and sip expensive cognac and tell stories. Because I had no heat, I sat at a local pizzeria and watched customers come and go with their pizza and ran into my old 6th grade teacher who I had not seen in 38 years.

Look how easily we can turn from grateful to greedy when things don't go as we expect. What if lights off actually meant that I shut the lights off and went to "sleep" earlier allowing myself to get more rest?

What if you could find the gratitude in the "unexpected" things that come your way?

What if you could find the gratitude in your bathroom scale? How do you react to what shows up on your scale? Do you get pissed off when it doesn't move down fast enough for your expectations? Have you experienced the joy of being ecstatic on the first week of a diet, when the weight comes off quickly? Then after that when the weight loss slows, do you start talking trash about yourself, your inadequacies, your "failing" to achieve weight loss success, and then do you quit altogether?

How many times have you stepped on the scale and complained in disappointment that you only lost one or two pounds? How often do the little thoughts in your head shout out, "I can't believe I only lost a pound, after being so "perfect!"?

What if you were to lose that baditude and replace it with your bad ass self? What if you took charge and said "I am so grateful for my health and that I am moving in the right direction, that I lost a pound and woo hoo to me? Wouldn't that feel so much better? Slow and steady wins the race. It's a marathon, not a sprint, and it is beyond freeing when you get off the roller coaster and coast your way to healthy and sexy.

Perhaps we've become desensitized by the national "big loser" television shows that have people dropping whole pant sizes in one day? Let's be real—it's friggin' television and surely you've figured it out by now that reality TV has no basis in reality. No one can live like that! They set you up.

Good food and fitness practices are important, but (smack!) patience and gratitude are even more useful, effective pieces of the weight loss puzzle. Patience is allowing your body to adjust to your new way of treating it well by feeding it well. You did not wake up fat one morning because you ate one cookie the day before. So why do you think you are going to wake up "thinner" because you were "good" for a week?

If I could credit one "idea" that built my muscles for my competition, it was being in the NOW. I only had four months so I could not focus effectively on the whopping 40 pounds I had to lose, I could not focus effectively on all the challenging training I would need to do over the 4-month period. It was a long way out, and scary. So, I decided to focus on the next meal and the next workout. I had only to stay present and focus on what was NOW, and I believed that if I did the best that I could at every NOW meal, that my body would show up as it should on that stage. And it did.

Gratitude is when you thank every single ounce. If you are not grateful for everything you have, trust me on this one: you are not getting any more good stuff. Good things come to those who are thankful. Even if you lose zero pounds one week, be thankful, you didn't gain two! When losing weight, your best course of action is focusing on this idea of "*being grateful, not greedy*". Hang that one on your scale.

Right at this moment, what are you grateful for?

_____

_____

_____

Perhaps it's your health; your life; your resilient body that will change when you fully participate in the process of getting "naked" with it, being kind to it, feeding it beautiful, pure and naked food, moving it, shaking it, dancing in it, celebrating with it, and loving it.

If you are present in your life, fully participating, fully experiencing all the moments as they occur, you are living in the "now." It is one of the most challenging things you can do, so you must work on the concept consistently. But when you do, voila:

awesomeness. I hate to break it to you, but the fact is, you really only have now. Even if you want to, you cannot go back into the past and change what you ate for breakfast this morning. So if you did not eat what you consider to be a healthy breakfast, the best meal possible at that moment, oh well; you might as well stop beating yourself up or obsessing about it. You can't change it anyway. What is the next meal coming up, and what can you do now to make it the best?

How many times have you had the thought and held it as true that: "If only I were thinner or richer or prettier, then I could be completely happy?" How many times did you expect something to happen when you got to that anticipated place, you made more money, you lost weight, you looked even more beautiful, only to find that emotionally nothing changed? You wanted even more, money, thinness, beauty; but you still weren't satisfied, and you still were not happy.

One summer, in what seems like another lifetime, I was packing luggage, my two baby boys (Randy, seven years old, and Mike, three years old), and a huge package of expectations into my car. We had struggled to save money, and I had planned for a road trip driving from New York to Orlando, Florida's, Walt Disney World. I planned and planned the easiest routes; how many rides we would be able to get on each day; what we would eat; what they would wear; the kids' glowing, loving smiles. Really, Rosie? I pictured the most exciting vacation with happy, smiling, cooperating brothers, dressed in matching outfits and oh, so cute! I wanted to be the happy family on the Disney TV commercials. I was living in the Disney trip months before I got there. Fully invested in what I considered to be the perfect scenario. But the universe had a different expectation of what perfect meant. "Are we there yet?" was the refrain throughout the 1100-mile trip and the saga began there.

My expectations for the perfect little two-and-a-half-kid, standard American family visiting Disney World with happy faces like the television sitcoms never materialized. First of all, there was a rainstorm (I think it was more like a tsunami), so the matching outfits that I so meticulously picked out for the boys were covered in sweatshirts that I was forced to buy—did I mention it was freezing in sunny Florida? Add to that the plastic poncho and, well, you get the wet picture. Alright, so get over it; it's just water. The rest of the trip was more like a trip to a "whinery." The boys preferred the hotel pool and lobby (and naps) to the Magic Kingdom's lines and let me know about their choice by whining, fighting, or sleeping through a long-awaited ride. Go figure. (There were no fast passes back then.) We were there, but it wasn't what I thought "there" looked like. The most memorable part of the trip was in the planning. The biggest lesson was to be less invested in the outcome and fully participatory in the now part of living.

What's my point in telling you this story, you ask? I say, don't think you are on a program by following the steps suggested in Sleeping Naked After 40. You are not. Sit down while I break it to you gently. There is no "there." There is only "now."

Now is the only time you have, so focus only on making the best of this moment.

Fall in love with the idea of taking care of yourself. You will never arrive at the place where you have taken enough care of yourself; you can never stop extreme self care, and why would you want to?

> *"You are, and will always be, a work in progress, and you need consistent self care."*

One day, when I was feeling overwhelmed by whatever was going on that day, I had a fleeting thought of "I can't do this." That thought was corrected immediately by a little prayer/affirmation that enters my head when I need it most. It is one that I repeat as needed because it will certainly crowd out any thoughts of "I can't" or "am I there yet."

This is my little correct-the-course prayer. Feel free to borrow it, and doctor it up for yourself.

"I will not give up or give in. I am safe, and I always have what I need."

Simple, quick, and effective.

You don't have a lot of time for the "poor me" saga. It takes time and energy away from the important stuff you could be doing.

In other words: Become less interested in why you can't. Invest in doing whatever it takes to get the results you want. Alright there may be days that you just want to feel sorry for yourself. Here's a little trick. Give yourself a set time (actually you can set a kitchen timer). During that time you have permission to be pissy, aggravated, irritated, annoyed. Then when the timer buzzes, call it quits on moaning. When the buzzer rings, get back to loving life. It's boring and old on that dark side of the timer. Who wants boring and old? Not you.

NUTRITION TRANSITION (Get your body in the game)

FAT CHANCE

Give FAT a chance. Give the right fat a chance. The healthy stuff that you have to eat for your health and your ideal body weight to show up. No one wants a "fat" body, but you do need to have "healthy" fat in your diet, such as:

- avocado
- coconut
- walnuts
- almonds
- flax
- sunflower seeds
- pumpkin seeds
- chia seeds
- hemp seeds
- salmon

You may be confused and frustrated by fat misinformation and not be able to decipher the truth about fat and weight loss. I can tell you from experience that I would eat one and a half avocados every day when preparing for the competition. Prior to that, in my "fake food," "deprivation diet" days, I would not touch "fat" with a ten foot pole (besides what showed up on my body), especially an avocado. Hell, I did not experience the joy of an avocado for forty years. I can tell you now, if you don't have fat, you will stay fat.

You can have these amazing foods listed above, and eat them, too. Pure, natural foods in their natural state—or as close to their natural state as possible. These fats are good fats. You need fat in your body to produce hormones, provide you with nutrients, and keep you flowing. Google "healthy fat" to confirm it further if you doubt this suggestion, and you will get all the proof you need to convince you that it is okay to indulge without any bulge when you eat them.

> *"Please don't say, "but aren't they fattening?" Eat the friggin' avocado and enjoy it!"*

I could be pissed at what I missed! I learned the hard way and am happy to share with you. If you are missing out, stop missing out. Eat the friggin' avocado and enjoy it. They are decadently creamy, satisfying, satiating, and yum. (Hint/Tip: Try something new, and spread avocado on your sandwich instead of mayonnaise.)

YUM. NAKED RECIPE:

AVOCADO BLUEBERRY SHAKE

This Avocado Blueberry Shake is made with delicious healthy fats and is a great pick me up breakfast or snack.

- 1/4 avocado
- 1/4 cup frozen spinach
- 1/2 cup blueberries
- 1 date
- 1 TBSP flax
- 1 TBSP chia seeds
- 1 TBSP almond butter
- 1/2 cup water

Blending this beautiful combination in my beautiful Vitamix makes me happy and in love with my food. After one week of eating this for breakfast, your pants will be looser, and you'll be a loser of weight.

are good fats. You need fat in your body to produce hormones, provide you with nutrients, and keep you flowing. Google "healthy fat" to confirm it further if you doubt this suggestion, and you will get all the proof you need to convince you that it is okay to indulge without any bulge when you eat them.

> *"Please don't say, "but aren't they fattening?" Eat the friggin' avocado and enjoy it!"*

I could be pissed at what I missed! I learned the hard way and am happy to share with you. If you are missing out, stop missing out. Eat the friggin' avocado and enjoy it. They are decadently creamy, satisfying, satiating, and yum. (Hint/Tip: Try something new, and spread avocado on your sandwich instead of mayonnaise.)

YUM. NAKED RECIPE:

AVOCADO BLUEBERRY SHAKE

This Avocado Blueberry Shake is made with delicious healthy fats and is a great pick me up breakfast or snack.

- 1/4 avocado
- 1/4 cup frozen spinach
- 1/2 cup blueberries
- 1 date
- 1 TBSP flax
- 1 TBSP chia seeds
- 1 TBSP almond butter
- 1/2 cup water

Blending this beautiful combination in my beautiful Vitamix makes me happy and in love with my food. After one week of eating this for breakfast, your pants will be looser, and you'll be a loser of weight.

I gave this recipe to a woman who, prior to hearing about "naked", could not lose weight, no matter what she did. In this specific week, the only change she made in her eating was adding this shake for daily breakfast, and when she came back to see me the following week, she had dropped two pounds. Woo-hoo!

OMG! It's so crazy delish! As well as nutrish! (There is a shake making video on www.cookingnakedafter40.com if you want to see first-hand how simple and easy it is).

This is your chance to lose some fat while having permission to eat some fat.

The fats you do not want to eat are these:

- butter and margarine
- partially hydrogenated anything
- oils (you can find as many arguments that oil is good for you as you can find arguments that it is not. According to the Sleeping Naked Doctrine, preference is given to the oil that comes out of the naked food. The foods listed above on the "good fat" list are foods that your body has to work on to get the fat from. Liquid oil, even olive oil, is technically processed and refined. If you choose to use oil, select top quality extra virgin olive oil. Be very, very wary of any oil that you get in a restaurant. Unless you are in a gourmet, chi chi, upscale place, chances are very good that you are getting an inferior food, probably cheap oil mixed with a little olive oil but labeled as olive oil. No kidding!

My newest and latest pet peeve is that "natural" nut butters have been attacked! Big food manufacturers who won't leave the pure stuff alone are up to their tricks again. They have taken to making "natural" nut butter by adding additional oils like palm and soybean oil. Why, you ask? The answer is so that you can stir it more easily as you grow lazier, fatter, and hungrier. I ask you, is it really that difficult to stir with a spoon? If you find yourself creating an excuse to use as your reason for buying the unhealthy stuff, I can help you with that - SMACK! If you think that natural peanut butter may rip the bread when you try to spread it - SMACK! With that I can offer a few options:

1. Spread the peanut butter on an apple instead of bread. The apple will not rip. It's just as satisfying and delicious.

2. Toast your bread and the heat from the toast will melt the nut butter.

3. Become less interested in your ripped bread and think about how you can have a

ripped, rockin' hot bod instead.

> *"Keep your BODY top of MIND when deciding what to put into it!"*

SMACK: (Get your head in the game)

~~"Pant Chants"~~ and ~~"Diet Speak"~~

Pant Chants and Diet Speak are not loving words. "Pant chants" are the scary monotonous repetitions of distaste and disregard for self. You know what I am talking about; the critical judging of your own body and the harsh words you use when talking about your precious self. You may be so good at this baditude and bad thinking that you aren't even aware how often the negative remarks about yourself fly out of your mouth. Remember what you mother told you and apply it here, "make friends and be nice". Make friends and be nice to yourself.

Your wake up call, jolt, shove, push or brain shift starts with a change in your self-talk. Doesn't it sound easy to just stop expressing those old negative, unserving, judgmental thoughts about yourself and replace them with better, kinder, gentler ones? It could be more challenging than that because it's been comfortably and habitually engrained in your psyche. However, you can change this way of thinking and behaving. It will take time and practice but it will be worth it. Like anything new, the more you do it; the more it will become habit and the better you get at it. When you become aware of what you are saying, only then can you begin to stop it.

> *"Every time you catch yourself saying or thinking something bad about yourself, acknowledge, forgive, rephrase, and move on"*

There are tools you can use to track your progress and monitor your body and weight fluctuations, progress and maintenance: pants and scales.

THE SCALE: If you can let the scale be a measurement of your success, not a definer of your worth, then it can be a good tool to keep you moving in the right direction. If you can accept that it is just a number and not make the number mean more than a measurement, then this can be a great tool for you.

You're in charge of this event and how you react to it. The goal is to find a way to measure where you want to be and the changes that are happening to your body, lovingly and kindly.

The bottom line is that deep down, you know your naked truth, and if you are not taking good care of yourself and nourishing yourself properly with the right foods, your know your actions are going to affect the number on the scale. That's probably why you fear stepping on it.

I have a very cool scale that has no numbers. Instead, it measures you according to your gorgeousness, hotness, sexiness and fabulosity. Step on this scale and you get a word to live into instead of number to piss you off. While leading one of my ladies' evening classes, I conducted an experiment. I told the ladies that it was weigh-in day and that they were required to come into the back room with me and step on the scale. Mean? Only a little bit. Let me tell you about the panic that filled the room immediately, and the looks of horror. Some women were visibly shaken. It was like I had given a death sentence.

The best part of the story is the ending. I was lucky enough to be in the room when they stepped on my special, new-and-improved scale that reported back to them that they were hot and beautiful, so I got to witness the delight, the relief, the laughter, and the joy that these woman experienced when they saw they didn't have to face the number. I actually got a few hugs. It seemed that whatever word they got, they were grateful as it had much lighter meaning than what they gave the number.

The scale stepping obsession can be a nasty business. There are some of you, and you know who you are, who step on the scale every day! Lord! Not a good idea. Step on it less often or don't step on it at all. The scale can be affected by a million outside influences, depending on the air you breathe, your salt intake, that extra spoonful of peanut butter. The realization that that number is always fluctuating can help immensely in dealing with the changes. So if this is you and if you find that you are affected negatively by the thought of a scale, you can stay away from it. No one demands that you use one. You may actually be better served stepping away than stepping on. If you consider scales a mood altering drug you can choose another option.

Just call yourself a "hottie" because that what my scale says you are.

You'd never walk around with a sign around your neck stating your number on the scale. Who really cares? It's how you feel that matters.

TIGHT or LOOSE CLOTHES?

For Option 2, you've got your pants. Experiencing your pants size changing, becoming better fitting pants that aren't digging into your belly and inhibiting your breath, proves that you are making progress. If you try on a pair of pants that fit last month, and they are tight this month, it's your warning that it is time to pull back and look at what you are, or maybe what you are not, doing for yourself.

Since you do walk around with your pants on (unless, of course, you are practicing your naked skills from a previous chapter), I suggest that you pick out a pair of pants that you wore comfortably at one point. By one point, I'm not talking about the pants you were wearing in high school or at your 25th birthday party. Okay? Don't be ridiculous here. I am talking about an attainable pair of pants that you wore when you were feeling at a good place. Here's a good rule of thumb: If the pants are out of "fashion style", for instance, the corduroy bell bottom lime green prints from 1970, they are not your measurement pants.

Pick the pair that you felt good wearing. Put them out on your dresser and leave them out, so that you can see them often as motivation. Pick one day of the week when you will try on these pants and see the changes in the way they fit. Let's call it "Sunday Pants." Remember not to make this goal ridiculous. If you are a size 16, wanting to be a size 2 because that was what you were when you were 17, forget it. (P.S. You'd look ridiculous anyway, and your head will look too big—who needs it?)

These pants will become your guide, your measurement (instead of the mood altering scale number) for having the ability to pull back just a little if you feel them getting tight. When you feel them tightening, stop right there—that's your cue to re-examine what you are eating. Right away. Don't get past those pants and on to the next size.

A client we'll call Patty, who lost fifteen pounds while working with me was looking great, eating really beautiful food, and loving it. Patty truly was at her ideal weight. But her head had not shifted and caught up to her transformed body and she found it challenging to find acceptance and self love at this point. She decided that she had to lose an additional five pounds and obsessed about it. No matter what she did, they hung on.

They hung on and she hung on to this idea that those last five pounds would have her fitting back in this one pair of pants. Those pants were chanting, "What about me, you're still fat without me." Lying, stinking pants wreaking havoc on her head. We had a conversation. All of her other clothing fit but that one pair of chanting pants, so I politely said to her, "Maybe you need to ditch those pants and buy a great new pair of pants that fit your new healthy, sexy (sustainable) body. You are at the place where you feel and look great, and now it's time to accept and appreciate how far you have come, and where you can comfortably be while being in love with your food and your body."

Your pants may fit better before the scale says you are lighter. That's a nice concept, let's go with it. Can you see how this is a head game?

More head games and pant chants that can drive you nuts—Are you thinking or saying things like this every time you walk into your closet:

My pants are tight—I'm so fat.
My clothes don't fit—I'm so fat.
I feel fat—I can't believe I let this happen again.
I have nothing to wear—I'm so fat.

I don't want to go out and be seen—I'm too fat.

I won't buy the next size up—then I'd be really fat?

Perhaps these pant chants will be the very thing that motivates you to start this journey, but once you start, you've got the chance to change your chants.

Take these pant chants and create a better use for them. Use these chants for more productive purposes than beating yourself up. Let's use these pants as a measurement of how far you have come. When they get tight: WARNING, pull back on how much you are eating or increase the amount of movement you are doing with your body. Either (and better still, both) will work.

Don't let the pant chants express any negative description of you. The fact that they don't fit doesn't mean you are bad, fat or have no will power. It means that they don't fit comfortably, right at this moment..

EXPERIENCE EXPERIMENT (Get your heart in the game)

Retrain Your Brain

Retrain your brain from diet speak to soft talk. Every time you catch yourself making a negative, diet, derogatory body comment to yourself or about your body or about your resolve, replace it by repeating a more positive sentence.

Document your changing "speak" this week:

I USED TO SAY (DIET SPEAK):	TODAY I SPEAK THIS WAY (SOFT TALK):
I was bad today at lunch.	I will make a healthy choice tonight for dinner.

For example, if you catch yourself thinking, "If I eat this, I'll get fat," or if you catch yourself saying, "I was so bad today," or if you catch yourself hiding because you "feel fat," stop. Replace your thoughts by making every meal count with good choices; replace your words by saying, "Next time I visit this restaurant, I will try the delicious arugula spring salad with blueberries instead of the pizza that I tried today. That will be a healthier choice."

Sleeping Naked After 40 167

Now for the fun part. Here's where you'll pay big time.

Every time you catch yourself using pant chants or diet speak, put a dollar in a can. When these dollars add up (and they will, in the beginning), you can treat yourself to something special—perhaps the chance to purchase a new rockin' hot pair of pants?

{ List 3 changes that you will implement in your life after reading this lesson:

1. _____
2. _____
3. _____

You've earned a rose.

LESSON 8

Become Less Interested In Why You Can't

Naked After 40 Vocabulary

Weight training:
The best exercise you can do for your body, head, bones and spirit.

Small steps:
Often thought unimportant, these small steps are giants in making change.

Become Less Interested in Why You Can't

What would happen if someone suggested that you couldn't take the time, or if you made up an excuse that you didn't have the time, to brush your teeth? That's simply would not be an option. You always find the time for tooth brushing. Now grant it, tooth brushing takes a lot less time than a workout but the point is that you don't think much about brushing your teeth. You just do it. It fits into your day without much thought. You don't agonize over it, you don't have to find time for it—you just do it. You fit it in because you want clean teeth, fresh breath, good dental health, and good heart health. That is the way you need to think about, and approach, exercising. There are 1440 minutes in a day. And you only need to take 30 of them for exercise, do that math. That's a very small fraction of your day.

> *"Fit exercise into your day if you want to stay fit and have a healthy body."*

You don't have to do a lot; you just have to do something. If you are doing nothing now, put your sneakers on and walk out the door.

After the figure competition, I was burned out and couldn't get myself back into the gym right away. My daughter said, "It's alright, Mom, even if you go for five minutes, just do something small." That was a big suggestion, and it worked. I listened, stopped beating myself up for not sticking to the "unrealistic plan" I had created for myself, and just did the best I could at the moment. If walking out that door and down the driveway and back is all you can do, then it's all you can do, and it's perfect for today.

Anything that gets you moving is a good thing. Each small step counts and will produce huge results.

Other than food, exercise is my favorite topic of discussion. Because I was brought up hanging around my father's homemade gym as he grunted, groaned, listened to loud music, and slammed the steel, I am a gym baby. My adult children are all trainers and bodybuilders and live in a world of fitness, food, and health, so we often discuss whether this was caused by nature or nurture. Whatever the origin, I am passionate on the subject of weight-bearing exercise and how important it is to your health.

I am a bodybuilder, not because I gained status by participating in a competitive figure competition but because I use weight training to build my brain and my body. I believe 100 percent in the power of weight-bearing exercise on your health and on your mindset. Weight training gives you the following (and these are only a few):

- improved bone mass
- a clearer mind
- toned muscles
- improved metabolism
- better sense of well-being and good health
- better appearance
- better performance

Once you understand the benefits of weight bearing exercises, you've got to do whatever form of exercise motivates and excites you. Participate fully, and make it count. Even if nothing excites you now, pick something and start the ball rolling. It will grow on you and become addictive over time, especially as you begin to feel better and see and experience the physical changes.

If you go to the gym, show up fully at the gym. Designate a set gym time for yourself, and get the job done. The hand-made sign in my son's gym says, "If you are in the gym, be in the gym". Don't take your cell phone or your baditude. Take your badass self and hit it. It's that important and that much more effective if you focus on what you are doing at that moment.

> *"Being "in the now" built my muscles. Being in the now will help build your healthiest, sexiest body."*

When I participated in my competition, there was a brief time when I needed to step up the pace and work out one hour in the morning and one hour in the evening. SMACK. I had to adjust my mindset and fall in love with the idea. I could not have done it if I did not love the whole experience.

Here's your movement prayer/affirmation (repeat it, acknowledge it, accept it):

I will age gracefully and with dignity, but I won't go down without a fight. I will not give up or give in. I will work on my strength and flexibility and movement, so that I can move and perform well in my daily life activities. I'll do it all to the best of my ability, just like I attempt everything in my life. I will put out the best in everything I do. Always doing my best will yield the best results, the best body, and the best me.

What do you want to do for body movement?

Do you have a favorite activity?

> *"It matters less what you do and more that you just DO SOMETHING."*

If you have no favorite right now, do anything that sets you in motion. Maybe you like walking, running, yoga, or belly dancing. Maybe you'll try NIA (aka: Non-Impact Aerobics, Neuromuscular Integrative Action, a sensory based movement practice incorporating martial arts, dance arts and healing arts), kickboxing, martial arts? Which one of these options works for you? Your answer may be different on different days.

> *"Maybe you just turn up the music and dance."*

"I don't know what to do," is no longer an adequate excuse as to why you are not moving. Get moving. Stop making up excuses and start somewhere. Straight out walking is safe and effective and affordable too. Put on your walking shoes and hit it!

The good news: if you are starting off with a lower level of fitness the opportunity for you to make improvements is HUGE. If you are currently doing nothing and start doing something, you will notice amazing results immediately. If you have been doing the same thing for a long time, you should probably switch it up and do something different. There are millions of ways to design a good workout program and as long you follow a few basic principles you will get results; a little bit of structure with a lot of room for flexibility to work with your schedule.

We'll start off with the most basic principles of training…

1) Progressive overload. Progressive overload is a gradual increase of stress on the body to cause specific adaptations. Basically, over-time you want to make sure that you are increasing some area of your workout. This is a gradual increase; it does not have to be EVERY single workout. The increase can come in the form of more repetitions, using heavier weights, doing a more complex exercise, increasing the intensity or even taking less rest time in between each exercise. Push yourself to make it a little bit more challenging when you start to notice that your body is getting better at it.

2) Specificity. Specificity states that the body will change in response to the way you train it. DUH. For example if you only do yoga, your body will become more flexible but it will probably not improve your mile time. If you only run and bike, you will become a better runner and biker, but it may not improve your bench press. This is where defining your goals comes into play. It will help you to figure out the specifics of your workout routine. For most of us, with the general goal of improving a couple of critical components of health (cardiovascular system, muscular strength and flexibility) we will have to incorporate different modes of exercise into our routine.

3) Variation. Variation is continually altering our training stimulus to prevent ourselves from getting TOO comfortable with what we are doing and to prevent our program from getting stale. Another no-brainer.

Fun Fact: For someone who is just beginning to weight train, their noticeable increase in strength and coordination in the first 6 to 8 weeks of training are due to adaptations in their central nervous system. Did you know that you train your nervous system?

Honestly, you can't put this off anymore. Your health is at stake; you can't sit still. Stillness is good if you are meditating.

> *"If you are sitting on your butt all day, that's bad. Not bad ass! Bad Ass women get their asses to the gym."*

When I use the word gym, it is referring to whatever kind of work out works for you. It is called a work out for a reason. Because it's work. If you are lolly gagging around, hanging on the machines looking pretty, talking to your friends, socializing and not sweating, you're not hitting it.

Finding what works for you is the only way you'll consistently keep up. If you are not at your ideal weight, you know it by the uncomfortable feeling that you have in your body. Your ideal weight is ideal for you because it's comfortable. If you see flapping flesh when you move, acknowledge it, don't hate it, but acknowledge where you are so you can move up from there. It's actually fun when you play a game with yourself and 'fall in love with the idea' of building your best body. Take before pictures of yourself, no matter how painful that feels at that moment, because it is one of the most motivational and inspiring ways to push ahead. Talk about a wake up call, a jolt, a slap, a smack. A block of wood hitting you in the head is what it feels like when you have to face that first before picture. Turn it into fun, as you watch your body change through pictures over time.

There's a big joke about turning fifty, that only fifty year olds know, because as a fifty-year-old, your eyesight diminishes, and it gets harder to see yourself in the mirror. You can maybe deny and ignore those little additional lines in your face that seemingly show up overnight. But not the thinning eyelashes that show up as hairs on your chin. Maybe the title of my next book should be, "Top Ten Unspoken Changes That Happen When You Turn 50." When it comes to your body, you can't step away from it. Even if you don't look in the mirror, your clothes don't fit, and you just feel like sh!t. Be honest. Feel it and do something about it.

In addition to the tightening of your pants, an overweight body doesn't move as well, and "things, pings, pangs, and pains" start showing up all over the place. Without exercise, you slow down physically. You lose strength and flexibility, and it gets harder and harder to perform even simple daily routines. You don't want to be that woman, that has a bowl fall on her head as she reaches up to get it off the top shelf. With no upper body strength to grab the bowl it crashes onto your skull? Nope.

You don't want to be that woman that falls and breaks a hip because she's got no lower body strength. Nope. So do something about it.

There is no hiding the naked truth.

I may be repeating much of this information about the importance of exercising but just as in the gym you repeat the exercise, the concept of getting movement into your daily practice is worth repeating.

Exercise and movement are essential to creating the healthy, sexy body you want. Years ago, when women stayed home and cleaned their own homes and gardened, they were physically moving and didn't need to have a destination location like a gym to get their physical activity in every day. Life is different today, with women working outside the home, immersed in this information technology–based, rushing, can't-do-enough society, where we are literally dragged and tied to computers from the moment we wake up. Couple that with the changes in and processing of our food supply, and you've got the perfect scenario for an overweight and unhealthy population.

REMEMBER, you need a plan that works. That means choosing an exercise that you love, one that fits into your life. It's got to be immersed in your life like brushing your teeth. You wouldn't go anywhere without first brushing them, would you?

What are you doing now? What could be better? What would need to change to make it better? Are you willing to do what it takes?

_____
_____
_____

Perhaps you need an accountability partner, someone to walk with, a gym membership, some group classes, a doggie to walk (borrow your neighbor's dog if you have to). Private clients participating in my Healthy, Sexy Body Weight Loss Experience tell me that accountability makes all the difference in the world. They pay me extra when they don't attend their weekly workout appointments they scheduled with themselves. Knowing that they have someone to report to, someone that cares, someone that they don't want to disappoint, keeps them on the right track. You need some accountability. Find it somewhere. A friend, partner, a trainer, a hired coach. Do whatever it takes to make the healthy changes you want in your life.

NUTRITION TRANSITION (Get your body in the game)

Naked Fuel

People ask me all the time if they should eat before or after a workout. Food is fuel; and the rest of the answer is not so simple. It really depends on you. If you are eating a great diet and are properly fueled all day, every day, your body will decide for you which way works best. I have had clients who need to eat before a workout (me) and those that feel sick if they eat before a workout.

Fueling yourself with good stuff is the most important thing. When you do that, it is less important whether you eat before or after. Now there will be gurus jumping out of the computer at me, saying eat thirty minutes prior to this and within thirty minutes after that, and that is like saying every diet works for everybody. It's about finding what works best for you, and if you are eating pure and naked and exercising consistently with focus, determination, and presence, your goals will be achieved, no matter when you eat your fuel. (Keep in mind that I said you must be fueling all day, every day, with the good stuff, using breakfast as your starting point—remember chapter one?) You can go back and reread chapter one again.

So what do you eat if you want to power up with a smoothie or a protein bar?

Beware of smoothie bars and counters. Most of the products they offer are filled with unnecessary ingredients and lots of sugar. What they promote as healthy food is really junk. You will be reversing your hard work by ingesting all kinds of sugar-laden garbage. There are tons of junky processed protein bars and powders out there that are nothing but candy disguised as health food. Beware.

One of my favorite food products is Brendan Brazier's VEGA Performance Protein. I just love this stuff. I used this product during the time I was training for my competition, and I still use it. It's very pure and green based, non-gluten, non-dairy, and non-soy. Brendan is a triathlete and a vegan and has created this product for those of us that want some protein but don't want to eat dairy and whey. I always prefer pure and naked food, however if it helps for a quickie snack—it is one of the best out there as far as powder is concerned. But you don't need protein powder to build muscles, pure and naked foods build healthy, sexy, beautiful, strong muscles.

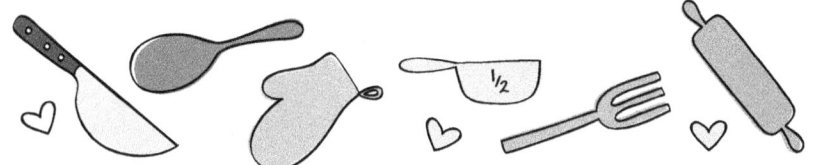

YUM. NAKED RECIPE:

CHOCOLATE ENERGY BARS

Here is a great, easy recipe that you can whip up and keep frozen to eat after (or before) your workout.

- 1 scoop Vega Shake and Go Smoothie (Chocolate)
- 2 TBSP peanut butter
- 1 TBSP raisins
- 1 TBSP pumpkin seeds
- 1/4 banana
- 2 TBSP coconut crème (see the recommendation list in the back of the book for where to find this product)
- Dash cayenne pepper
- Sprinkle sea salt
- Sprinkle cinnamon
- 2 TBSP water

Mix all together in a high-speed blender.

Spread out one inch thick on a piece of wax paper and freeze.

This recipe makes two bars. This is yummy good and tastes like a decadent fudge bar.

NOTE: There is a resource guide in the back of this book, so you have the opportunity to see how to order my favorite things.)

SMACK: (Get your head in the game)

Replace Disappointment With an Appointment

The most important appointment you'll ever make is the one you make with yourself. It's a non-negotiable appointment. You must show up to the appointment if you want the body of your dreams to show up for you. An appointment with yourself is the surest, most effective way for deterring the disappointment you will feel when you don't get your workout in.

If you have been currently doing nothing and have no idea where to start, you can start by stopping yourself from making a big deal out of this. Walking works. Simple walking. One foot in front of the other, plain ole' walking. Put on your sneakers and walk out the door. Walk five minutes in one direction and turn around and come back. You've walked for ten minutes and can congratulate yourself. Tomorrow, do six minutes out and six minutes back. Now you've done a total of twelve minutes. Keep on adding a minute or two every day. Before you know it, you'll be up to thirty minutes a day, and that's nice! I set the time on my phone for fifteen minutes and walk out the door. When the timer chimes, I walk back to the house. It's that easy. No thought involved - no big deal, but big results.

A client we'll call Dianne, wanted to weigh eighty pounds less. She could not get herself motivated to get to the gym, she felt weird and awkward about going and she was doing nothing physical. She lived at the top of a very long, steep driveway. Everything seemed overwhelming, out of reach and near impossible. How would she get started? I suggested that every time she went out to get into her car, she walk to the bottom of her driveway, touch her mailbox, and walk back to the car. She thought this was fantastic, a fun game, a challenge and she agreed. Dianne said confidently, "I can do that," and she did. She proudly reported back to me how many times she walked up and down her driveway. Then she started to walk around the lake, and then she started to report how she walked two miles. It's addictive, it feels good, it puts you in control as you are doing something physical and making a difference in your health without the big hoopla of having to get to the gym. Walking is sustainable, and that is your goal — **sustainable and implementable changes and strategies that work for the long term and for your life.**

Walk with an attitude, a bad ass attitude. There are other reasons to walk besides the physical benefits that walking brings. My Grandma Violet was very consistent and persistent when it came to her daily walk, that she called her "daily constitution." Walking can become a meditation and a chance to connect with your body, to the earth as you feel firmly planted on the ground, and a chance to open up your mind with silent thinking time. Walking allows you to slow down, think, and exist only in the moment. Focus on the ground and move forward, step by step. Think of walking as a step-by-step process of getting closer to your goal. You need no special equipment or gym membership. Just get your butt out there.

You've got to MUSCLE UP AFTER FORTY, not slow down.

Hate to break it to you ladies, but as we age, our muscle mass deteriorates and gets replaced with fat. Lovely thought, right?

You can do something about it.

Weight training increases muscle and decreases fat. So which one would you prefer? (check out some exercise vids and what you can do when you get to the gym on www.sleepinnakedafter40.tv)

It's guaranteed that your pants will fit better when you start lifting some weights! 5 pounds of flabby fat takes up more room in your pants than 5 pounds of lean muscle tissue. Just saying.

Strength training is the key to staying fit. **Having a plan that is sustainable matters more than anything else.** It matters less what you do and more that you just do it. Being consistent is better than being consumed and obsessed with working out; obsessive strategy burns you out. That is not taking extreme care of yourself. It's not all or nothing; instead, it's getting something done every day. Don't start with a ridiculous plan to work out at the gym for two hours, seven days a week. You know you can't keep that up (nor should you), so why set yourself up for inevitable failure? Why not set it up so that it works for you, your life, and your body? Twice a week is all it takes to get health-promoting benefits from weight training—huge benefits like weight loss, strength, flexibility, mood enhancement, and stress relief.

What if you could walk into every room like it was your party? How would it feel to own that room because you felt so good in your body?

> *"Nothing you eat can make you feel as good as toned muscles and a leaner mass make you feel."*

You feel sexier, and you look it, too. Your skin is tighter and glowing, your posture is straighter, your pants fit better, your strength is evident. The bottom line is that you feel amazing, knowing you are taking steps and doing something.

Fall in love with whatever idea you have for bringing exercise and movement consistently into your body and life. Find what you love, and make it work for you. Whatever you decide to do—whether pilates, yoga, zumba, a combo—it is recommended that you participate in planned movement two times a week. Consistency is key.

I have found what I love and, more importantly, figured out how to make it work for me. My gym is ten minutes from my house, and I can walk there in any weather if I have to. I also prefer to work out in the morning, so I schedule it into my calendar as an appointment, and I get it done. My yoga teacher lives in my neighborhood, so my class is easy to get to; and that **reduces the excuses**. I make it an easy, habitual, consistent part of my life.

How can you implement simple strategies that will work in your life?

Where do you need to go? How far? Can you seek out new places in your neighborhood? Is someone holding small intimate classes in their home?

There is definitely a lifestyle part of the workout equation.

"Lifestyle" exercises are the movements you do without a planned gym or program. What is it that you like to do: dancing, cleaning, gardening, walking the dog…? And they count.

Before you do anything, ask yourself one question. "Is what I am doing moving me in the direction of my healthiest, sexiest self?" If you can answer "yes", go for it! If the answer is "no", you need to consider doing something different.

LIFESTYLE ACTIVELY CHART
Think about how you can incorporate more lifestyle activity into your daily routine. Make a list of at least two ways. Be creative!
1.
2.
3.

Can you?

- park your car farther away and walk to your destination?
- use the upstairs bathroom when you are downstairs?
- take the stairs instead of the escalator?
- walk to errands wherever possible?
- do your own lawn and gardening?
- do sit-ups or pushups while watching television?
- walk over and visit your neighbors?
- get up and change the channel?
- walk the dog?
- walk your neighbor's dog?

On their own, these things don't seem to make much difference; but added together, they keep you moving, and that is empowering. Incorporating some or all of the "lifestyle" suggestions will change your life. It's an added cushion to support you in keeping you viable, flexible, and healthy. Get off the couch and move it, baby.

How do you make a plan and a goal to incorporate fitness changes?

You become a S.M.A.R.T.I.E. P.A.N.T.S and begin making sustainable changes that fit in your life. Each one of these letters represents a strategy that you can use to work towards making your fitness goals permanent.

S.pecific: You've got to know exactly what you need to do, with details. Don't get to the gym and walk around cluelessly about what to do. Hire a trainer, take a class, but have a plan.

M.easurable: You gotta see results. Goals should be recorded and reassessed periodically. This can include the scale, body fat measurements, pants assessment, a journal, full body pictures (I know you love that- but just think how awesome it is that you are taking your BEFORE pix and the after pix is closing in) You then check back on this exercise choice in three months and adjust and readjust accordingly.

A.ttainable: The goals should be attainable and do-able on a consistent basis, meaning not too hard and not too easy. Don't be crazy with your goals and burn out. You want this to be a real life change, something that fits nicely into your life.

R.elevant: The goals must be relevant to your interests, needs, and ability. You must be in love with what you are doing. It's a mindset. Change your mind. Fall in love. When you walk in the gym, smile and think grateful thoughts that you are healthy enough to show up in a gym.

T.imely: Goals should have a specific deadline for completion. Breaking it down into small goals and a weekly schedule is a great way to take it slowly and consistently, so that results show up. Can you choose an event, a photo shoot, a marathon? It's fun to have that goal but now that your life goal is your health, you will never stop wanting or creating health for your body.

I.mpactful: Your goal should have a positive impact on your life and how you show up in it. Your exercise can be low or no impact, and still the result is impactful to your life (again I stress, that it is your body, you know it best, so tailor your fitness goals to meet your capacity).

E.ducational: Your goals should teach you to be better and better.

P.ersistence: You must be convinced with every cell in your body that you can and will do it. As Napolean Hill so eloquently states in his chapter (and my fave) on Persistence, "Be Persistent no matter how slowly you may at first have to move. With Persistence will come success."

A.ttitudinal: Your attitude has to be a positive and your head and thoughts have to be in the game. Release your baditude and embrace your bad ass!

N.othing: Let nothing stop you or stand in your way. Go over, under, around or through, whatever it takes.

T.ruthful: Be sure that you ask yourself if this is an honest goal; one that you really want and one that you are willing to take on wholeheartedly.

S.imple: Notice I did not say that it was easy because it may not be easy but it does have to be simple so that you can get it done. If you create complicated, dramatic situations, you will burn out and quit.

> *"Is what you are doing moving you in the direction of your healthiest, sexiest self?"*

EXPERIENCE EXPERIMENT (Get your heart in the game)

Grow Yourself: Create your Personal Development Plan

Take a loving look at yourself in the mirror. Don't be judgmental or critical. This is your chance for deep honesty. Ask yourself if you are taking the best care of yourself possible.

I promise you won't die by opening your eyes and looking. You may be surprised. You may be shocked. And you most likely will be motivated to do something.

When all else fails to motivate you to move, this getting naked trick works. Do you look the best that you can look?

_____

Are you really taking proper care of yourself, now that you are learning how that is possible?

_____

Here is your mission and your experience like no other:

Get Naked and stand in front of a full-length mirror. Take a good look at your body—front, side, and rear—and say HELLO. There is no ignoring what is facing you. This was hard work to get naked in front of the mirror and the work will continue with step by step care that will change your physical shape and your mental state about how you are thinking and perceiving your physical body. It is possible that you do not drop a pound but still fall in love. Who's to say what will happen when you put your pieces together?

But now be nice while looking into this mirror. Remember that you are the fairest of them all. Pick a body part that you have been picking on and find a reason to love it. If you were glaring at a jiggly thigh, start to think about how lucky you are that your strong thighs can walk you through the neighborhood or carry you to the gym. Take that one body part and continually and consistently think good things about it. Love it fully, embracing all of it.

Your body has an ideal weight. It is the weight where your body feels comfortable and is at a weight that you can easily sustain while eating pure and naked food. It is not the weight that you were when you were nineteen. If that's what you are thinking, you'll need to adjust your expectations.

Here you have it - one more thing to hang on your refrigerator door:

For the next week (date_____), I commit to exercise by _____on the following days:

DAY	TIME	DECISION
(ex) Monday	12:00–12:45	Meet Kate and walk

(I will list these days and times on my calendar and keep my appointments with myself) FYI : This appointment is just as important as the one you make with your doctor. Act as if it's that important. As a matter of fact, it's even more important, because this date with the gym can actually keep your doctor visits few and far between.

Signature_____Date_____

Setting your twelve-month fitness intentions (and breaking them down). This will provide a guide that you can look back on and acknowledge your progress.

What do I plan to change in the first three months?
_____
_____

in six months?
_____
_____

in nine months?
_____
_____

in one year?
_____
_____

How will my body be different in six months?
_____
_____

How will my clothes fit in six months?
_____
_____

What has to change for me to keep up with my committed, persistent, sustainable workout schedule that is just as important as brushing my teeth?
_____
_____

How committed am I to reaching these goals? (scale of 1–10, with 10 being the extreme, all in, no matter what, rain or shine commitment)
_____

Thank and love your current bod, while also envisioning and welcoming the new one at every step of the process. Here's a great exercise that worked for me.

Cut out a piece of heavy card stock the size of a dollar bill. Imagine you are living in the body of your dreams, with confidence, attitude, sexiness and love. What's that feel like? On one side of the paper, write a description of the FEELING you have when you are feeling and experiencing the confidence, attitude and sexiness. Search through some magazines and paste pictures on the other side. These pictures can be of a person, body type, dress you want to fit into, outfit you want to wear. Each image should conjure up the body you want for yourself.

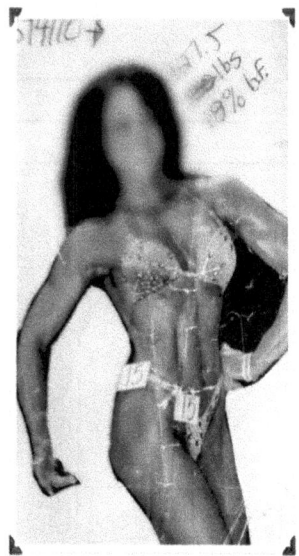

I did this exercise about 7 months prior to entering a body building competition. I did it long before I actually made the decision to enter a body building competition. It just so happens that the picture I subconsciously chose to represent the way I wanted my body to look was the picture from a workout magazine and a figure competitor posing. Cool huh?

Low and behold, the picture and the weight number I chose were almost exactly what showed up for me. As a matter of fact, I think I looked even better than the girl in the photo. How's that for "building" the body of my dreams! You can too. Have fun with this.

*One more very important weight loss tip to consider.

Do not write these words on your card... I want to LOSE _____ pounds.

Instead use this different approach and write on your card:

I weigh a healthy, sexy _____pounds.

List 3 changes that you will implement in your life after reading this lesson:

1. _____
2. _____
3. _____

Another rose for you. Purchase a single rose today, and honor yourself for moving that beautiful body in a beautiful way.

LESSON 9

This And That

Naked After 40 Vocabulary

Patience:
The capacity to accept what comes, knowing that it <u>will</u> show up.

Persistence:
Obstinate continuance in a course of action.

Perseverance:
Steadfastness and stick-to-it-ive-ness.

Amazing proportions:
The result of putting the above pieces together.

If it's not this, it's that.

I love "this" and I love "that" too, but when you are using this and that to create an excuse, well, that's just plain ole' crazy. I'll tell you "this': you'll never get anywhere with "that" baditude. When I hear someone trying to convince me of an excuse that they have turned into a reason for not doing something, I recognize it right away. SMACK. I don't have much patience for the excuse thing. There are always thousands of excuses but never a very good reason. I inform my clients on day one of my mantra for them and for myself which is, "I am not interested in why you can't; I only believe that you can." I believe it for you, right now, even if you don't yet embrace it for yourself.

An excuse usually starts with a confession of not doing what you intended to do, because "something" came up. Now I am not saying that you are a liar; I am saying that excuses are the lies you create in order to justify why you don't do something. "This" something got in the way of doing "that." As I see it that "that" was your choice. You see, "**I can't** can be substituted for **I choose not to**." That little slip of language can change everything. Start substituting the words and see what transforms before your very eyes. If you tell yourself, "I can't go to the gym, substitute and replace it with: I choose not to go to the gym" you will see how different and powerful (or powerless) that statement makes you feel. Everything will change.

An excuse is just an opportunity to stay where you are. Is that acceptable for your amazing, extraordinary life? What are you missing out on accomplishing because of an excuse not to do it?

_____

_____

What excuses can you identify right now that you are using to avoid living to your full potential?

_____

_____

What excuses are you making for not losing the weight you say you so desperately want to lose?

_____

_____

You invested time and money to read this book because you are not willing to stay where you are.

There will always be something that gets in the way of your plans, distracts you, slows you down. That is the nature of life. We deal with things. It's how we deal with these pop-up things that makes the difference. It's how we deal with our "this's" and "that's" that matters. That is the game of life, the ebb and flow, the cause and effect, the "yada, yada" (yes, I am and always will be a Seinfeld fan).

If it's not this, it will be that. There will always be something. It comes down to what you make of that "something."

> *"An excuse is an opportunity to stay where you are."*

If you accept and embrace this idea that life is made up of challenges and lessons, you can get through them with grace. Just like the weather outside, sometimes it rains, sometimes it pours, but the sun always comes out tomorrow. We know that and expect it. Even through the rainiest, snowiest, stormiest blizzards, the rainbow and sun will come up in the end.

NUTRITION TRANSITION (Get your body in the game)

Your Power Prescription

Your only prescription is to take action. You need a plan to have good food to eat, so that you won't attack anything that isn't nailed down. Being prepared is crucial to successfully eating for health. If you are not prepared, and you are starving by your next meal, you will grab whatever is around, no matter if it's good for you or not. No amount of willpower is going to save you. I've been known to grab whatever is not nailed down when I am starving. The solution is to have something good to grab. The feeling of hunger will surpass any willpower that you may have for making good choices. The options get slimmer (and you'll get fatter) if you grab whatever.

So how do you prepare to always have a healthy option at hand? Here are my suggestions for getting yourself ready for any situation that may arise.

TRAIL MIX BAGGIES

Fill up a bunch of individual-sized baggies with nuts, seeds, and goji berries, and leave them around—in your desk drawer, your purse, your car. These come in handy in any emergency situation when you need something to keep you going.

VEGGIE CRUDITÉS

Have some bags of veggies cut up and ready to grab when you walk in the door and need something to snack on: raw carrots, string beans, grape tomatoes, broccoli.

SHAKE UP

Have a healthy shake option that you can mix instantly. Frozen fruits mixed with a scoop of almond butter in a high-powered blender have a great frozen dessert consistency and make a satisfying snack or mini meal.

FROZEN STUFF

Have bags of frozen vegetables in your freezer. It takes minutes to prepare frozen spinach by sautéing in a little vegetable broth or coconut oil or plain water sauté with seasonings.

DESIGNATE A NAKED COOKING DAY

Designate a day to cook once and eat for days.

On this day:

Bake a bunch of sweet potatoes. Sprinkle with cinnamon and wrap in foil. Bake at 350° for 45 minutes or until soft to squeeze. These are great warm or cold and last for days in the refrigerator.

Make brown rice and quinoa mixed together. Use a rice cooker, and you'll have no worries. You can eat this yummy mixture sprinkled on your salad, as a side to your lunch or dinner, or as a breakfast cereal with added nuts, dried fruit, and warm almond milk. It will stay fresh for at least four days.

SLICE AND DICE

Have containers of sliced and diced carrots, onions, mushrooms, and celery. These chopped veggies can be added to your omelet, your turkey burger, atop your salad, or as a starter for sautéing a dark leafy green vegetable.

> *"You need a plan to have good food to eat, so that you won't attack anything that isn't nailed down."*

YUM. NAKED RECIPE:

YUM-AZING FUN POP

Measure out 2 cups as your portion. Package in small individual serving size snack bags and save the rest for other people or other days.

- 1/4 cup cashews
- 1/4 cup pecans
- 1/4 cup raisins
- 1/4 cup extra dark mini chocolate chips
- 8 cups popped popcorn (organic popped on stove with one tbsp coconut or grapeseed oil)

Mix altogether for a treat. If you put the hot popcorn in with the chocolate it will melt onto the popcorn for a delicious taste. Either way you do it, this mixture is yummy and fun. Pop in a movie while you're at it and really treat yourself.

SMACK: (Get your head in the game)

On and On

Don't make excuses. The fact always is, when you are 100 percent committed to getting something done, you are gonna do it; there ain't nothing gonna stand in your way. You go over, under, around and through to get it done if it needs doing.

That feeling of 100 percent commitment is the feeling you need to conjure up in assessing any situation.

If you are able to come up with an excuse to not do something, you need to look at the reasons you are not willing to give it 100 percent. It may be something you really didn't want to do anyway, because if you did want to, you would.

The results are in your choice, your commitment. It's as simple as that.

> *"Develop an attitude of 4 P's: patience, persistence, perseverance, and planning."*

If it's not this, it's that, is just the way life is. In speaking with a friend, she complained how tough her week had been. She went on about how she had hurt her knee, was stressed over her daughter, money was tight…and on and on.

She could have done things differently by picking out a few positive things about her life and switching the focus to them. This is not an easy task at first, but it is a much better way of viewing life. Your perception is everything, and you have control of how you look at any situation. You can make yourself feel good or you can make yourself feel bad, simply by changing the way you think about things.

There will always be something popping up in life that, if you allow it to, can set you back and keep you stuck from moving forward.

This is where you can take charge of a situation. You don't have to let anything stop you. You can change the story that keeps you stuck in Excuse-Making Land.

I will further share my experience as an example. I set my heart and mind on a specific goal, (you know, the bodybuilding contest). Yes, it had been a dream of mine since I was a young girl of twenty. Instead, I had babies and raised my family and never got to my bodybuilding dream. I can list many excuses why I didn't do it and why I could never do it. I share this story because I learned so much through this process. When I decided to finally do it at fifty, I had to make an adjustment in my baditude that would not allow those excuses to permeate and destroy what I wanted to do. I did not want to look back in ten years at the "woulda, coulda, shoulda, poor me, now it's too late" stuff.

I had a small window of opportunity—four months to lose forty pounds and 15 percent body fat. No one (including my food coach/show prep trainer) really thought it possible, and they told me so. No one believed I could except for my children and my own inner desire that raged stronger than any doubt. I fueled the flames of I WANT THIS consistently, persistently and took the actions that were necessary to produce the outcome I desired.

Once I made the decision, I made it fully: no looking back, no doubting, no listening to what anyone thought. I planned, persisted, and persevered. My focus was always on the next step I needed to take. I took the next step, no matter what. I didn't let anything stand in the way of what I wanted.

That is the attitude you need to develop to get anything done. This is bad ass!

Together your 4 P's are powerful: planning, patience, persistence and perseverance will pay off when you use 'em.

That's how you do it. You keep going, no matter what. You tear down walls. Go around them, go under them, go over them, go through them. Don't turn any excuse into a reason.

Sit for a moment and remember a time in your life when you accomplished something of amazing proportions that was outside the realm of realistic possibility, but you just persisted and persevered and made it happen?

When was that time?

_____

What did it feel like to accomplish your mission?

What did you have to do to make it happen?

What is it that you want so badly now that you will would be willing to take whatever steps necessary to get it?

What area in your life that is not working the way you want it to?

What is the ~~reason~~ excuse that you are not doing something about it?

Now you have acknowledged the excuse, let's make a list of what would have to change in order to excuse the excuse.

Your goal is to get rid of the "this or that" mentality and replace it with "that was then and this is now." Rephrase it to say, **"Now I am empowered to make the changes necessary to achieve the results that I want."**

Then (meaning yesterday), you were an excuse person. You were the type that maybe (often) was stopped by some event, person, occurrence or thought. But that was then and this is now….Now (starting at this moment), that has changed. You are focused only on what you do want, not on what you don't want.

You can and will persistently and patiently, with perseverance and a little planning, move toward getting what you want.

Ask yourself again, with this SMACK and new-and-improved brain shift:

What do you want for your life?

_____

_____

What are you willing to do to get it?

_____

_____

EXPERIENCE EXPERIMENT (Get your heart in the game)

Lose the Excuse (and the weight will follow)

Where in your life are you making up excuses that keep you stuck?

List one area.

_____
_____

List three excuses for not getting this "project" completed:

1. _____
2. _____
3. _____

What is the benefit to you for not accomplishing this "project"? (trust me, there is one. If you dig deep enough, you'll uncover it)

_____
_____

What would happen if you were to accomplish this thing that you desire to do?

_____
_____

What are you afraid would happen?

_____
_____

Is this fear realistic?
_____
_____

What will happen if you don't accomplish this goal?
_____
_____

The Real Deal

We spoke about the real deal being the real naked food that you eat. But there's more to that story. That is the real you. So what exactly do I mean by that? I mean, who is the real you in that mirror. Who is the person looking back at you? When was the last time you really looked at her?

Mirror Mirror on the Wall

One day when my daughter and I both agreed one mirror in my house was more flattering (okay, made us look thinner) than the other, we decided that beauty is in the eye of the beholder. Others see how you project yourself, but while that image is skewed by their personal background or biases, confidence always shows up as beauty, no matter what size you are. When you are caring for yourself with good food and self care practices, you glow from the inside out and that beauty pours out of you and is infectious to others. You reflect what you are feeling on the inside.

One of the fun things I like to do is put on some red lipstick and kiss the mirror. My lips are marked on the mirror and make me smile every time I look into it. I believe that one of the joys and benefits of being over 40 is that your eyesight is, let's say, not as sharp. This allows for a gentler look, a soft lens look, at yourself in the mirror. When standing in front of the mirror. Go easy (no picking). Be gentle (lose the harsh words). Don't judge (stop the criticism). Just love all that you are and all that you are not.

Change your look(ing) by taking a plain hand held mirror and sparkling it up. You can buy an inexpensive mirror and glue in the dollar store. Glue the back and around the mirror with old broken crystals, jewels, pretty shiny stones. This makes a handy dandy tool when you need to be reminded of your specialness. It makes you feel royal and appreciated and pretty, like a princess. And why not!

> *"When I turned 50, I knew it. I became a princess and not just for the day."*
> *~ Rosie Battista*

List 3 changes that you will implement in your life after reading this lesson:

1. _____
2. _____
3. _____

Your reward for a job well done is to buy yourself a bouquet of the most gorgeous flowers available. Brighten up your space with nature.

LESSON 10

What's On Your Plate?

Rosie Battista

Naked After 40 Vocabulary

Your plate:
Either your physical plate that holds the amount of food you eat, or your life plate that holds the amount of stuff you have going on.

Dainty dining:
The way a princess would eat, nourishing yourself like royalty, serving on nice plates, enjoying the meal because you deserve it; or simply taking princess-sized bites of food.

TLC:
Tender Loving Care.

How big is your plate?

Are you overfilling your plate? Someone once made a comment that stuck in my head. She said, "You are a beautiful woman, measuring 5 feet 4 inches. If you are feeding your body and eating like a truck driver, you're going to create a body that is like that of a truck driver." SMACK, now that made complete sense, but I had never thought of it that way. If you are eating enough to maintain a 200-pound body, you'll maintain a 200-pound body. If you are eating enough to maintain a 140-pound body, you'll maintain 140-pound body.

How do you eat?
- Standing up?
- Driving in your car?
- Picking?
- Skipping?
- Rushing?
- Inhaling?

If there is so much on your plate (the life plate) that you don't have time to eat a plate of food with dignity, then small steps need to be taken and big changes need to occur. If you are busy taking care of everyone else and don't have time to nourish yourself lovingly or dine while focused on your meal, something needs to come off your plate.

What size is your plate? How much is heaped on your "life" plate (your to-do list, your self-care list)?

NUTRITION TRANSITION (Get your body in the game)

NAKED EATING

Eating becomes spiritual when you clean up your act. When you choose "God-like" food, (food as God made it) or food that is as close to its natural state as possible—pure naked food—the nourishing experience becomes spiritual and divine. You will be less likely to abuse food in any fashion when you are spiritually connected to it.

In the previous chapters, we discussed what to eat and the importance of eating green, real, unprocessed foods. Hopefully, you have put into practice some of the suggestions I made on adding more greens, getting clean, and being selective about what ingredients go into your body.

What you eat is mighty important, but how and when you eat make a difference, too. Dainty dining supports the concept that "the body is the temple of the soul" and houses all your goodness and love. The way we treat ourselves around food and nourishment is a reflection of how we love ourselves.

You have lots of opportunities to nurture and care for yourself, as you eat at least three meals a day. This is where you can show yourself the TLC that you deserve.

DAINTY DINING (with a Candid Camera crew at your table)

If a video camera were focused on you as you ate, would it be pretty picture? Now, that's something to chew on.

Overeating, under-eating, and eating poorly are all forms of violence against ourselves. When we begin the act of dainty dining, and self-love is the goal, there is no room for eating toxic foods (even if we eat them daintily) or eating healthy foods in an unhealthy way. There is only room for love.

Use my Dainty Dining Rules as a guide for being kind to yourself, and eating in a loving, nurturing way. Once you've embraced Dainty Dining, you can invite that Candid Camera crew in with confidence, at any time, and they will witness your self-love and capture the proof that you are providing extreme self-care to the one that matters most—your precious body.

Rosie's Dainty Dining Rules

1. Eat mainly pure, naked foods like fresh raw fruits, vegetables, nuts, seeds, beans. Take into account seasonality and local buying. Appreciate the joy of biting into a crisp red apple in October or a juicy peach in June. Support and sponsor a local farmer by buying produce from a neighbor. Invest in a CSA share or even share a share with a friend. CSA is Community Supported Agriculture. Depending on your agreement, you might pick up a weekly box of farmer-selected produce from your local farm. And that means you will eat ultra-fresh food, with all the flavor and vitamin benefits. And you will become acquainted with new vegetables and new ways of cooking. Look for a local CSA farm at LocalHarvest.org.

2. Before eating every meal, pause to express gratitude by saying grace or a few brief words of appreciation both to the food that is nourishing your body and your body for its health, vitality, and resiliency.

3. Take small bites, and put the fork down in between.

4. Chew slowly. Practice by counting to twenty and making the food last for at least twenty chews.

5. Shut off your phone, your computer, and your TV, leave the book in the study and focus on your food, savoring each bite and each delicious flavor. Be mindful of what you are eating.

6. Reduce the size of your plate, fork and spoon (try a demitasse spoon). Use any tools that will remind you to pay attention to portion size. Other ways to "Go Small" include using a demitasse cup or shot glass for beverages and condiment bowls or dainty bone china tea cups for soups and sides.

7. Remove the serving bowls from your easy reach. Try leaving them off the table entirely, perhaps keeping them on the stove, so it is more of an effort to get more. This will give you a few seconds extra to realize you may not need an extra helping.

8. Try chopsticks. If you are not a pro at using them, they can slow you down and minimize the size of each bite you take, making it near impossible to gorge yourself

in a feeding frenzy.

9. Try filming yourself while you eat and see where you could slow down and eat more daintily. (Use your smart phone). You may want to dance like nobody's watching, but eat like the whole world (including the royal family) is. Think about the first time you went out to eat with a love interest…maybe all the way back to high school. Remember how you ate differently maybe because love was in the air. Well, maintain that love every day, by loving yourself, your food and your body.

> *"You may want to dance like nobody is watching but eat like the whole world is watching."*

YUM. NAKED RECIPE:

DREAMY NAKED CHOCOLATE FUDGE

- 2 cups pitted dates (soaked for 2 hours in water and drained)
- 1/4 cup dry oats
- 1/4 cup walnuts
- 1/4 cup raw cacao

Mix all ingredients in a Vitamix or high powered blender until smooth and scoop onto wax paper in one inch balls. Put the tray into the freezer until balls harden into fudge like consistency.

SMACK: (Get your head in the game)

Get Down to It

When I was eating with my husband, whose build was much bigger than my small frame, I noticed how much he ate. Lots of times, it was less than I ate. The difference showed up on my body as extra pounds. I figured out that watching him was a way for me to measure my portions and gauge my speed eating. Was it necessary for me, a small woman, to devour the same amount of food as a large male? Of course not. Eating for your body is a simple concept that you can use to judge the situation on your plate.

Using tools can aid in helping you monitor how much you eat. Adopt the tools that work best for you. If you practice with them, they will change the way you eat, and that will change your physical weight. But that's not all. These tools allow you—force you—to experience eating differently and mindfully. They help bring the connection between you and your food into focus, acknowledging that you are eating to nourish yourself. They also prevent you from unconsciously shoveling in the food as you are racing to get the meal over with and move onto the next item on your "To Do" list or trying to beat out the rest of the diners to make sure you get your fair share.

The Secret Six for Successfully getting DOWN to Naked Eating:

1. Slow down: Take human-sized bites and chew them. It's as simple as that. Engage in the process of counting for twenty chews. See how close you can get. Breathe before you take another bite.

2. Fork down: Put the fork down in between bites. I was particularly reminded of this one day when I was lunching with a friend. We both ordered the same salad. She took a bite, put her fork down and chewed. I, on the other hand, was shoveling the food in like it was the last meal I would ever eat. Once I became aware of what I was doing, I began to slow down. That's a great way to remind yourself. Watch your meal partner. If they are eating slower than you, chances are you are rushing; take heed and slow it down. If they are shoveling, become aware of what that looks like, how unbecoming it looks and how unnecessary it is. For the most part, no one's threatening to take your plate away.

3. Calm down: Meditation and prayer are another set of powerful tools that aid in slowing down the overeating process. When you connect with the spiritual source, eating becomes a spiritual practice and one to be honored, appreciated, and completed with care.

4. Lie down: taking a nap, not eating. Lots of times we think we are hungry, but actually we are just tired. If you take care to rest when you are fatigued, you'll stop those episodes of eating for the wrong reason.

5. Write it down: Keeping a food journal helps you see clearly what you are actually eating. It also may aid in stopping you from eating too much, because you don't want to write it down in your pretty journal. But you must commit to being honest with your journal regardless how ugly your entries (or should I say "entrees") are, for it to work its magic.

6. Sit down: Make mealtime special. Sit down and eat. Never eat standing up. If you could eat only when you were seated, what would happen? You would delete a lot of unnecessary, unwanted calories from your day without trying or ever feeling deprived.

Make each meal special by using plates, cloth napkins, tablecloths. I have a collection of gorgeous small plates - different-sized cake, salad, and bread plates to match or enhance my moods. I serve myself on heart-shaped dishes, especially when I am eating alone, so I can remember that I am loved and to nourish myself with love. Add pretty glasses, flowers and candlelight, soft music. Savor the ambiance as much as the food. Make dining an experience of love.

Develop your own set of dainty dining practices. Which of the rules, tools, and suggestions will you use to apply to your next meal?

1. _____

2. _____

3. _____

EXPERIENCE EXPERIMENT (Get your heart in the game)

The Chocolate Challenge/The Body Challenge

PART I - THE CHOCOLATE CHALLENGE

> *"Don't make eating chocolate a bad thing. Lose that baditude. Chocolate is awesome, naked and sexy. If you eat it correctly, it can be a badass experience."*

Imagine taking one small .5 oz square of dark chocolate and make a lasting impression by making it last, a long time? How cool would that be? Now you may be thinking that you could never just eat one small piece of chocolate and be satisfied. But that is the old you thinking and your baditude showing up again. The new you, the bad ass you have become, can do anything she sets her mind to. She can change her thoughts with new awareness and an experience. This is an exercise in pleasure and in patience.

NEW THINKING AHEAD: What if you ALLOWED yourself this special treat with no guilt attached to it? Would that permission process be the motivation for you to choose not to eat the whole thing in one sitting?

Maybe you are one the few who felt she could NEVER resist the whole thing. But that was before you learned to really eat with all your senses and experience the joys of chocolate and slow-eating?

Try your Chocolate Challenge. First, you'll need to purchase some Dark Chocolate of the finest quality you can find and afford. Have fun with this. Shop around, research the chocolatier, the company, the company mission. The finest dark chocolates will give you the most satisfaction and the most health benefits. Remember to read the ingredients (of course by now in this lesson number ten, you know what the frig' you are eating) A good dark chocolate will have a very high percentage of cacao. I am talking over 70%. So that is your goal. Look for any dark chocolate made with over 70% cacao. Try brands like Green and Black organic, Dagoba, or even Lindt, which are readily available in most supermarkets and malls. But there are decadently more gourmet delites to whet your palate. Picking the best dark chocolate is purely subjective but the basic premise would be to select one with minimal and "naked" ingredients. There is the potential added benefit in picking the best possible chocolate: the expense (sometimes up to $15 a bar), may in itself limit the amount of chocolate you can afford, so you'll want to make it last. Relishing darker dark chocolate is a process of initiating your taste buds to experience its complexities, especially if you are used to drug-store quality milk chocolates.

Allow your preferences time to change and practice your patience as your taste buds grow into your new way of eating and caring for your body.

Let's begin the "Chocolate Challenge", an experiment in patience and pleasure:
1. Unwrap the chocolate - look at it. How does it look?
2. Hold it between 2 fingers, as your body temp warms the chocolate feel it soften and melt slightly. How does it feel?
3. Smell it. How does it smell?
4. Hold it to your ear. ~ Do you hear anything? Most likely not, but it may be speaking to you and calling your name to take a bite. Just that very thought of it so close to your mouth may produce a salivating sensation.
5. Finally place it in your mouth, on your tongue, but don't let your teeth touch it.

At what point did you notice that your mouth started to salivate?
Were you satisfied with that one little square?
What did you learn about yourself and the chocolate during this experiment?
What was your experience while eating dark chocolate like a lady in a dainty way?
Did the chocolate seem different when experienced with all 5 senses of looking, smelling, touching, listening, really tasting?

PART II - THE BODY CHALLENGE

Write a letter to your body about your food and the relationship you have with it. (I know, I have asked you to write a lot of letters in this journey. Some may have felt more comfortable than others. These very letters that make you feel the most uncomfortable, the one's that you resist most, are the ones that are the most important for you to write).

This letter should address some food-related thinking or thing in your life that is no longer serving you. Maybe it's your need to "over" eat or "under" eat. Here is an opportunity to identify the negative, old relationship, you had with your food. This affirming letter to your body is where you can tell it whatever you wish to say in a kind and loving way. If you over-feed your body or treated it badly through food choices, now is your time to come clean. Be free, clear, and honest in your letter. Get it out of your gut and express your feelings to your body.

Use this sample letter to start your writing flow, and complete the sentences with your own feelings.

(ex:) Dearest Body of Mine,

Thank you for being so resilient and for putting up with my_____ during our prior relationship.

I'd like to change that part of our relationship. This is how I want our relationship to look._____

This is how I would like our relationship to feel_____

Since we are together so often, and you are part of my every moment, moving forward here is what I propose_____

I promise to do my best each day to nourish you with healthy, beautiful food in a loving way by practicing _____. I affirm that you are_____.

xxxooxx, Love,

_____(put your name here)

Now, doesn't that feel great to fix up the relationship with the body you are carrying everywhere with you? Your body will respond beautifully (and show up sexy and healthy) in response to proper nourishment, movement, and your added TLC. It wants to be healthy and it will show up when you give it the opportunity.

While you are thanking your body, you may want to consider acknowledging your "other" brain as well.

YOUR OTHER BRAIN

The standing joke about men is that they think with a body part other than their head. Well, guess what, girls? We ladies do the same. We have another powerful brain that we sometimes try to ignore. Oh, but this body part will have no part of that. It will not be ignored. It's rather insistent in its desire to get your attention when it knows something is out of whack. This brain is your gut. Your gut speaks to you often. Butterflies, knots, aches, rumbles, pains, pings, and pangs are all cries that you need to pay attention.

Have you noticed that your gut has a "mind" of its own? This is not just a figure of speech, it's really true. There is something called an enteric nervous system or ENS. Your ENS is powerful. It is located in the tissues lining the esophagus, stomach, small intestines and colon. This amazing network of neurons (100 million of them) has the power to learn, to remember and to give you "gut" feelings. Just like your larger brain in your head, your "gut" brain receives impulses, records experiences and responds to emotions. It can play a major role in your happiness and state of wellness.

The butterflies in your stomach are talking to ya. Are you listening?

Describe a time in your life when your "gut" spoke to you, told you to do or not to do something, and you chose not to listen.

_____

_____

What emotions were you holding onto in that gut?

_____

_____

What messages was your gut sending you?

_____

_____

Recognize how smart and fortunate you are because you have two brains working for you. Are you prepared to listen, closely. If your stomach tells you that you have had enough, listen to it because it doesn't just talk about food.

BELLY BASHING

In my informal poll of women I know and work with, it's pretty evident that the belly is the "winner" of the most disrespected and disliked body part. It's too big, too squishy, too jiggly, too bubble-shaped, too saggy, too lumpy – you name it.

Muffins may have a place in this world (check out my healthy muffin recipe in my Cooking Naked After 40 Cookbook), but it's not around your middle. If you are eating processed, refined foods, they will show up on your body, most likely around your belly – there you have your cause and effect.

THE CORE CONCEPT

In countries around the world, the belly is an honored body part and considered the center, cultivating life force, and power. In Japan, the belly is considered the home of the soul or hara. In China, the belly is referred to as the Gate of the Mysterious Feminine.

CONNECTING TO YOUR CORE

Your belly is your core. In exercise, and most movement modalities, weight lifting, yoga, pilates, you are instructed to work on your core. All power comes from your core and that is where fitness starts. Your core is your trunk and it holds you all together.

Women ask me all the time how I got my abs. They assume that I do millions of sit ups in my workouts. I assure you that I do not, way too BORING for me. Even during my body building competition, I did minimal sit ups. The strong flat abs and rips that showed up for me, showed up because of my decision to eat "naked". During my regular, non-competitive life, I still maintain a mid-section that does not puff over the top of my pants like a muffin, or as I call it a "popover".

Want a great fun, sexy way to improve your core strength and connect to your core – try belly dancing. You'll get to wear a jingly scarf around your waist that sings to your movements.

> "A woman is closest to being naked when she is well dressed."
> ~Coco Chanel

BELLY BELTS

If you find yourself "hating on" (that's a phrase used often by my daughter or the Gen Y's) your belly, it's time to readjust your thinking. You can start with the food you feed it (pure and naked), and the attention you give it (a sexy, subtle or not so subtle belt or scarf), some attitude (be proud of it), and some gratitude (find the good things that you love about your belly by remembering what it does for you).

Decorate your belly. Belts have come a long way from a necessity back in the day when their sole purpose was to keep your pants up. Today belts are expressions of our style sense and our personalities. And as much as they are now worn for fun, they also have a "Naked Purpose". Belts help you remember that your belly is the source of your feminine beauty. They help keep you on your naked path – Too loose means "way to go!" Too tight means "whoa".

I am a self-confessed fashion fanatic, making and designing outfits, retro-fitting clothes, and acting as fashion consultant to my ladies who lost their unwanted pounds. So let me tell you about belts. Belts, glorious belts, are part of the reason I need an organized walk in closet. As a collector, from classical to comical to flirty to jewel encrusted, I own an Elvis belt, a skull and crossbones belt (to look bad ass, so if you see me wearing that one watch out, I don't take any crap or excuses from anyone.)

If you absolutely refuse to wear a belt right now because you feel you have no waist or can't find one that fits comfortably, another fun thing you can do to bring love to your core is to dress it up. Purchase removable tattoos (available in drug stores or accessory stores) and decorate your belly, or you can take a (safe) magic marker and draw a heart on your belly. Only you know that it's there. How fun and sexy is that? It will make you laugh and remind you to care for her.

WHEN FAT IS WHERE IT'S AT

If you have fat building around your waist and belly, your health is in trouble. According to the medical community, it can be a dangerous marker of internal grumblings.

CORE ESSENTIALS

Here are the 4 core essentials for caring for your center core:

1. Trust it (listen to your gut, your butterflies, your knots, your central knowing)
2. Embrace it (adorn and appreciate your belly, exactly how it is right now)
3. Acknowledge it (be grateful for the strength and centering that comes from your core)
4. Nourish it (naked food will help your belly feel and look better with every bite)

BELT IT OUT

Remember what my coach said when she encouraged me to "Walk into every room like it was my party". As I reflected on this mission, I actually started to become aware of how I walked around my world and presented myself to others. I figured out that she was correct and if I was going to walk into any room, I might as well walk in as my best self. Hell, it's way more fun when the party you're going to is yours! BREAKTHROUGH MOMENT: How about walking into every task and adventure as if it were your party?

You're far enough along in this book right now that I want to be sure you understand key concepts. So what does "being your best self" really mean? Do you know? Think about it before reading my definition. Being your best self means loving yourself enough to take good care of yourself (through implementing all of the strategies talked about in this book). If you are practicing these new or forgotten ideas, you can and will have the confidence (and attitude) to show off your good stuff. And hey baby, your good stuff is amazing.

> *"The lesson here is that when you hold back your good stuff, the real you, your "naked" self, you are depriving the world of your gift."*

If you make this conscious decision to walk around "differently", to walk with confidence, you won't even need a belt. Because confidence is the only accessory you ever really need.

With confidence you upgrade to become a Rockstar. Here is your list of what it takes to be a Rockstar.

1. A Rock Star does what it takes to be the best she can be.

2. A Rock Star does NOT make up excuses for why she CAN'T.

3. A Rock Star makes each step the best step towards the direction of her dreams.

4. A Rock Star only believes that she CAN.

5. A Rock Star accepts challenges as a learning experience.

6. A Rock Star is committed, dedicated and persistent.

7. A Rock Star knows that when she deviates from her plan, she can and will get back on track.

8. A Rock Star is always learning, moving and shaking.

9. A Rock Star knows that when she's got health, she's got personal power.

List 3 changes that you will implement in your life after reading this lesson:

1. _____
2. _____
3. _____

You've earned a rose.

LESSON 11

You Deserve It

Naked After 40 Vocabulary

Self-esteem:
Knowing and accepting your own worth and beauty.

Confidence:
Knowing and accepting your own worth and beauty.

Sweet options:
Involves planning and creating routines and practices that sweeten your life in non-food-related ways.

How much can you do, without doing yourself in?

There is a missing piece for most women over forty. That missing piece is self-care. Taking time out for ourselves is something we don't think about, allow, or give ourselves permission to do. We think it's lazy.

My mom (68 years old) mentioned one day in conversation how guilty she was feeling. When I questioned, "About what?" she responded that she did nothing all day except read her book. I asked if she enjoyed it and liked what she was reading. "OMG!" she responded, "I loved it all!" She was beating herself up for relaxing for one day, and even though she is retired and doesn't have children or a family living with her, she wouldn't (or felt she couldn't) give herself permission to slow down and enjoy. Part of this is taught to us—how to act, how to care for ourselves, putting everyone and everything else first and then feeling the guilt if we don't abide by our own made-up rules. The only person judging my mom was my mom.

It's time to make choices, take control and schedule a date with yourself. On this date, you will do whatever you want. You have permission. So if reading all day makes you happy, then read all day. If planning a full day of relaxation seems too much, set a time and take an hour or two.

Steps for making your date with yourself happen:

1. Embrace it (accept that you have the right to this time alone)
2. Time it (give yourself enough time to fully enjoy it)
3. Love it (fall in love with the idea of spending time alone with yourself)
4. You deserve it. (Just go with it)

There are some not-so-extreme things you can do that will have you feeling extraordinary. Pouring loose tea from a beautiful teapot into your favorite china tea cup with a lace placemat, baking up some delicious scones for a treat with your tea, and pouring your tea and sitting with your journal.

If you actually had a chance to sit and think for a moment about only you and what you wanted for your life, how would that feel?

_____
_____

Let's imagine that you set a time and you had to do something fun in that time. Start slow and allow fifteen minutes a day. Keep adding to the time. Set yourself up as I suggested with a cup of tea, a scone, and a pen and paper. Give yourself the opportunity to tune into yourself, to dream, to brainstorm, to journal, about what you love. What would you be doing if you could do anything?

_____
_____

Be wild, be creative, be extreme. No one is going to see this but you. What do you want? You have permission to write it down. Nothing is too grand for your one very precious life. What is it that you really want?

_____
_____

You may elect to dress up for this date with yourself. Put on your favorite anything. Maybe you choose to stay in your toasty warm pajamas all day, because you never get to have that experience, or maybe you choose to slip into one your best dresses, just so you feel rockin' hot, because you never get to have that experience.

Alright! YIPPEE! You've come so far, ending up here in lesson eleven. You know by now how I feel about the white stuff. I am hopeful at this point you are feeling the same way. YUCK. So there is more that I want to add to the list of bad white stuff: you already know to lose the white refined flour, sugar and sh*t you "used to" eat.

Now lose the white underwear.

If you have white cotton underwear in your drawer... throw those frumpy things away. I mean really? You're a gorgeous, healthy, sexy rockin' hot superstar, so act your part (not your biological age).

Run to the store ASAP.

In your adventure to lose the white - be wild, be extreme. Get yourself some passion purple panties, a rockin' red hot thong or leopard print trimmed with pink lace hiptsters. The fact that no one knows you are wearing your pizzazz makes it that much more exciting. It's a great way to start to "live into" that sexy lady that you are. Enjoy the process as you become more and more sexy, confident, bold and fearless with everyday that you work on yourself.

> "Seriously, you've got to start acting and feeling sexy to become sexy."

Your sexy feeling will improve your day. Just get out there and purchase the sexiest, prettiest pair(s) of undies you can find.

I don't care if you think you aren't in the perfect shape just yet. To hell with that. You need to know that right at this very moment, right here in Lesson 11, you are perfect for today. Live it NOW. Act as if you already have the body of your dreams. Treat it that way.

So get your butt to the store and get those rockin' hot panties!

It may be a secret that only you know about. But how fun!! And why the frig' not! What are you waiting for? Hmm? If there is no there, you've got NOW to make the difference. Whether or not you feel your body is ready for such an "X traordinary" treat, just do it and do it now.

PS. Even though you are sleeping naked, you need clean underwear for the day. (My mom used to say, and maybe yours did too, "make sure your underwear has no holes, just in case."

What you wear matters. But what you feel matters more. And when you are dressed up you feel UP!

If you are walking around in ratty sweats all day and feeling dumpy, you are immediately putting yourself in that same dumpy state of mind and mood. Private schools did the research and put mandatory dress codes into place because for a reason. They figured out that if students are dressed to respect themselves and honor their school, they behave better, more like students, less like bums.

You don't ever have to act your age, as a matter of fact I hope you don't, but you do have to act the part. Who is it you want to be? If you are in the process (and you are if you are reading and participating in this book) of building a healthy, sexy body and feeling rocking hot, then you need to dress with the look of rockin' hotness. I'm not talking about exposing the girls, flashing thighs, baring tummies. Those actions look too desperate. I mean look, feel, act and step into your gorgeousness.

When you are dressed to feel rockin' hot, powerful and confident, you will experience the feelings you thought you lost. I am about to tear down one of your excuses right here and right now, and I can sense you're all coming up with them. So just stop it right now if you are in the mind space of "I don't want to buy NEW clothes because I am still losing weight". Here's the solution to jump that hurdle very inexpensively, and in no time find yourself in a new outfit.

Check out your local thrift store or garage sale. And it's fun too. Spend a couple hours searching around (this can count as part of your self care time)

I have gotten gorgeous designer clothing from perusing local thrift shops. I consider it treasure hunting. In fact one little treasure I found was only $2.50. It's a form fitting teal crushed velvet dress, with a slit up the side. As a matter of fact I wore it on stage at a speaking engagement and got so many compliments.

I wear a piece of "olde" in everything I do daily. It's become part of my signature style, either a pin, a scarf, a dress, a coat, a purse. I just love the feeling of vintage. Shopping thrift helped me discover a part of myself that I hadn't realized existed. What do you love? What makes you feel special? What is your style?

So take the opportunity and "fall in love with the idea" of going on a hunt for the most gorgeous, inexpensive get up you can find! Find your style and your clothing voice.

You may just discover what your signature look really is.

Maybe it's
- a scarf
- a bracelet
- a necklace
- a color
- Or a belt…remember those?

Maybe you dress for tea. Invite a friend to share a scone with you.

Now, you will not be answering your door with your sweats on will you?

Create your golden opportunity to put on your beautiful dress and you'll be able to say to a friend "why my dear, I dressed especially for our time together and in celebration of our friendship. Because you are worth it! And because why the frig' not!"

Why own beautiful clothing and jewels just to leave them sitting in the closet? What are you saving them for? Use your good stuff for yourself. If you save your gorgeous clothes only for that designated "special" occasion, what does that say about the special time you spend with the special you?

And another thing…

Remember to get out the good china. There is no saving for a better day, use it NOW. Use it everyday because every day of your life is special and you are worth it.

> *"Don't save the good stuff for the company of guests - use it for the company of YOURSELF."*

With your table set to the nines with linen and china and your favorite tea and your body adorned lovingly with your new "style" of dress, tea time is an event worth attending.

NUTRITION TRANSITION (Get your body in the game)

Treat Yourself Well

Just because you cook naked and eat well does not mean you can't have delightfully delicious homemade blueberry scones. These yummy scones that taste like you walked to the nearest bakery take only thirty minutes to make and bake.

YUM. NAKED RECIPE:

BLUEBERRY SCONES

These make-and-bake blueberry scones are pure and naked. OMG! and there is no white, refined, flour or sugar in these delectable babies.

- 2 1/2 cups almond flour
- 1/2 tsp baking soda
- Pinch salt
- 1/4 cup coconut oil
- 1/3 cup coconut cream
- 2 eggs
- 1 TBSP vanilla
- 1 cup frozen blueberries

Mix all wet ingredients (except for the blueberries) in a bowl. Mix dry ingredients in a separate bowl. Combine wet and dry ingredients until mixed and fold in frozen blueberries.

Scoop into 1/4-cup rounds on a baking tin and bake for 20 minutes.

These yummy scones freeze well, so you can bake a bunch, wrap them up individually, and grab 'em when you crave 'em. These divine treats have no white flour and no sugar added, but that doesn't mean they aren't adding some sweetness to your life.

Top off with a steaming cup of loose tea, and you've got heaven on your kitchen table.

Loose teas of yummy flavor combinations can be purchased at www.artoftea.com. My faves are the dessert teas; especially, but not limited to the **chocolate monkey** (chocolate, banana, rooibos (when fermented this plant is the source of red tea; it is found in South Africa and is full of phytchemicals and anti-oxidants), pink peppercorn and **banana dulce** (chamomile, roobios, lemongrass, banana, and coconut). Oh, and don't let me forget to mention the **blueberry cheesecake** tea. Most of these teas are caffeine free, so will not interfere with a good night of sleep! Allow yourself a special treat and fifteen minutes to sit down and enjoy it.

> *Get out your favorite tea cup and your loose tea and set the table for "thee".*

SMACK: (Get your head in the game)

Make It Up to Yourself

At this point the only thing you should be making up about yourself is your face. If you are making up stories about how you don't, won't or can't look good until you're at your perfect weight, it's time to ditch that baditude. And it's time to make yourself over. Because feeling good NOW, accelerates your weight loss journey. You deserve to make it up to yourself. You know they give free makeovers at most department stores. You can't even tell yourself you can't afford it.

While you are purging your old thoughts of not being ready for your new face, purge some of that old makeup that's been hanging around growing bacteria.

When was the last time you bought a new lipstick?

For God Sake Woman, throw that crap out and run to the department store. You don't need a lot of bucks for this activity but it is a great part of feeling well. Stop those lips from talking badly about you and gloss them over with a new color.

I love the beautiful shiny gold tube of Chanel lipstick which is described on Chanel's website as "intensely rich in colour with a sumptuously soft, velvet matte finish".

Holding that tube makes you feel divine and special. These little gems come to you in living colors of L'Exquise, La Fascinante, L'Exuberante, La Ravissante, and La Sensuelle. See what I mean? You feel decadently deliciously sexy already, don't you?

Pretending that self-esteem and confidence aren't tied to how you feel in your body, about your weight, and about your physical appearance, is a lie. They are all tied together. I've never met a fat, out-of-shape woman excitingly jumping up and down rejoicing about how fat and out of shape she is. Nope.

Building your healthiest, sexiest self goes beyond what happens in the gym. Your body fights for balance and wants to live at its natural and ideal weight. That is where it is most comfortable. After the competition, my body desired to have a few pounds back on it, and I happily obliged.

Accepting where you are and feeling beautiful at every age and every stage (and situation) is growing older gracefully. There will be fluctuations, a little up shift, a little down shift but within limited fluctuations. It is true that the inner strength, the core, the belief, the feeling, the knowing that you are doing all the things necessary to "build" the best you that makes the difference.

> *"It's FOCUS. It's FAITH. It's INNER STRENGTH. The 3 pillars to successful, sustainable health."*

Take this moment to remind yourself of the accomplishments and positive changes you have made with your food and your attitude:

List 3 things that you have learned about your food:

1. _____
2. _____
3. _____

Your body:

1. _____
2. _____
3. _____

Your life:

1. _____
2. _____
3. _____

Yay for you! Congratulations!

EXPERIENCE EXPERIMENT (Get your heart in the game)

What's on Your Menu?

Treating yourself well should be something you work on daily. Decide what that means for you. Treating yourself well and adding sweetness to your life does not mean food and sugar. All you need are fifteen minutes and a timer. Sit down and do something for yourself.

What does that look like for you?

_____
_____
_____

Would you read a trashy novel, a sexy magazine, a food magazine, doodle, draw, sculpt Play-Doh, journal (Your Naked Truth Journal, hmm, hmm, written by ME, but filled in by YOU, to help you get your thoughts out of the recesses of your brain and onto paper), watch an old movie, scrapbook, meditate, dance, sing?

I like to sit and pet my pug. He is so adorable and groans with pleasure when I pet him. I'll give him ten minutes and a little massage, and he is in his glory and I in mine as he adds a dose of sweetness to my life. Where in your life can you give so that you can get some added sweetness without sugar?

_____
_____
_____

Start your list, which we will call from here on out the menu, of "sweet" options so you can refer back to them and choose different ones on different days.

_____
_____
_____

When my daughter and I were preparing for the competition, and had a time commitment for getting our bodies into shape, we had to focus on something other than food for fun. We realized during this four-month period that so many activities revolve around food. We decided to incorporate something special that we could do for ourselves that did not involve eating. We chose manicures, pedicures, movies, museums, and walking, drawing, painting, scrapbooking. It was amazing and fun to come up with other things to do besides going out to eat. What options can you list for yourself that involve something other than food?

_____
_____
_____

Create your own Soul Nourishment Menu.

What can you put on your menu that will nourish your soul and fill you up in ways far better than food? When you are hungry it may not always be for the food on your plate. You may be hungry for Soul food.

What is the #1 food that makes you feel happy when you eat it?

_____

What kind of memories does it conjure up for your?

_____

List 3 favorite healthy snacks that satisfy you and that you love eating

1. _____
2. _____
3. _____

List 3 things you love to do. These are things that get you so absorbed that you forget about time when you are doing them.

1. _____
2. _____
3. _____

List your 3 favorite tea flavors:

1. _____
2. _____
3. _____

Who are 3 "long lost" friends that you would love to have time to talk to but haven't yet created an opportunity for that to happen?

1. _____
2. _____
3. _____

If you could do something crazy and unexpected, what would that be?
_____

What kind of project(s) have you been wanting to start, but never seem to get to?
_____

List your 3 top favorite movies of all time?

1. _____
2. _____
3. _____

List 3 steamy, exciting, juicy or sexy novels you have been wanting to sink your teeth into?

1. _____
2. _____
3. _____

Make a list here of all the people that will benefit from a happy, healthy you, so you can see the importance of taking these extra moments for yourself and making yourself happier:

1. _____
2. _____
3. _____

{ List 3 changes that you will implement in your life after reading this lesson:

1. _____
2. _____
3. _____

What is your favorite flower? Buy it for yourself today

LESSON 12

Sleeping Naked

Naked After 40 Vocabulary

Sleeping naked:
Feeling comfortable enough in your own skin and loving your body enough to show up fully in your life. No playing it small or hiding like a wallflower because you don't like how you look in your own skin.

Sleeping Naked

It wouldn't be right to end a book titled Sleeping Naked After 40 without talking about sleep. I guess leaving it for last proves that it is one of my biggest challenges and one I have worked on (and still work on). You need sleep to dream well, function and perform optimally during the day.

My mother's actions taught me that sleep and napping were lazy and unacceptable. When I was a little, my siblings (three sisters) and I would go to bed. We'd go off to LaLa Land leaving mommy behind with a bolt of fabric and her sewing machine. When we woke in the morning, there would be 4 matching dresses sewn and made hanging in the kitchen. Sometimes there would be five, if she made one for herself in the same color, so when we went to church we were a matching family unit. There were the vivid orange spring coats that all five of us wore with white dresses adorned with orange daisies under the coat. Another time there were navy wool capes with gold buttons. Again all five of us marched into church, with my mom carrying the extra baggage under her weary eyes.

This was normal to me, and anyone who went to sleep at night and actually wasted time sleeping was lazy. My mother never stopped, never rested, never stopped cooking, creating, working, preparing, inventing. I spent years staying up all night working on projects, thinking I was doing a good thing. I thought of sleep as an annoyance and a waste of precious time that I could use more productively. I adopted her belief that sleeping was useless time, and so the longer and later I stayed awake, the more stuff I could get done. Just like my mom. It was a long time before I could change that belief and create a system and a plan around my sleep that would make it a special part of my self care practice.

As a child, I actually counted sheep at night. I was unaware that it worked like a form of meditation and would shut down any scary thoughts I was having, as I was too busy counting. Inevitably, after saying "hello" to thirty of the wooly souls, I would fall asleep.

Where does your sleep pattern come from? What were you taught as a kid?
_____
_____

What does your sleep routine look like now?
_____
_____

Sleeping well, (just like eating well and exercising well), is a super important piece of the self-care puzzle. So important in fact that if you have trouble getting enough of the right kind of sleep, you need to plan and create a practice and ritual to bring sleep into your life. Similarly to altering your eating habits, your sleeping schedule requires consistency, practice and persistence.

If you are sleeping as you should, you would be spending approximately 1/3 of your life or about 20 YEARS SLEEPING so don't you think it would be wise to consider how you can improve upon your sleep routine.

First, don't skimp on your mattress, your sheets or your bedding. You spend a lot of time in that bed, so make it count and be sure to get the highest count bed sheets you can find and afford. Secondly, do not take electronics to bed. Take only your happy thoughts, your gratitude journal, your loving partner (if you are lucky enough to have one) and your naked self.

NUTRITION TRANSITION (Get your body in the game)

Don't Be a Bag Lady

There is nothing more unattractive than bags under your eyes from lack of sleep. Ask my Mom, who carried those heavy things for years. Setting up a routine and creating a ritual that works will lull you to sleep, bring you to LaLa Land a little easier. If you struggle with sleep, it is crucial to create a plan that is consistent and routine, so that your body adjusts.

GET SOME SHUT EYE – THE RITUAL PART 1

- Pick a time. There's a reason moms give kids a specific bedtime, they, like you, need sleep and making sleep a focused part of your life improves intelligence, memory and promotes weight loss.
- Tea time is a nice way to mark the end of a day of eating. Try any kind of tea that supports relaxation. Yogi brand teas have a selection appropriately named "Bedtime", Celestial Seasonings Tea has one called "Sleepytime". Whichever tea you choose, make sure it has no caffeine.
- Power down and unplug from electronics before bedtime - the TV, the computer, electronic games - as these all stimulate the mind before bed.
- Settle down with a book or mindless magazine for at least thirty minutes before bedtime. Read gently (not a murder mystery) when you get into bed. I made the mistake one night of reading a novel about the daughter of a hangman. Needless to say, after I was done reading about the gory hanging that went badly, I had some dreams that went badly. Read something soft, gentle, sweet, inspirational, loving. Leave the other stuff for the beach.
- Add some lavender spray or essential oils to the room. In old folklore, pillows were stuffed with lavender flowers to help restless people fall asleep. Studies

confirm that the scent of lavender has calming, soothing, and sedative affects. I keep lavender essential oil by my bed and massage it on my neck before I get into bed at night. Lavender is useful in reducing feelings of anxiety and stress. Lavender essential oils are awesome, and there are plenty of lavender sprays that you can spritz onto your sheets. Take a warm bath with Epsom salts and lavender oil to begin the restoration of tired muscles and to begin the slow down before sleep, and breathe.

- Lose your thoughts and drift off to sleep to the enjoyment of soft music or a guided meditation CD.
- Figure out how food fits into your nighttime ritual by conducting the experiments below.

The debate about eating before bedtime.

Experts disagree on this; whether to shut down at 6pm or have a bedtime snack. In my expert opinion, the key is not to overstuff before bed. If you are eating healthy all day, meaning that you are eating pure and naked, it doesn't much matter when you eat. Your body will dictate that to you, so be listening.

Feeling uncomfortably stuffed is never a nice feeling, especially before bed. I love what Dr. Joel Fuhrman (my mentor and truly the real deal when it comes to nutritional excellence backed up by the science to prove it) says: if you eat until you feel your stomach, you've eaten too much. Your stomach is an organ, just like your liver, spleen, or kidney. You don't go walk around feeling your kidney, do you? You feel your stomach when it's in distress, too hungry or too full, or just plain sick. Remember to listen to your stomach, it's talking to you.

Test your body. Do you sleep better when you go to bed slightly hungry, or do you sleep better when you have a light snack before bed? Everyone is different. There is no right answer here. The goal is to get a good night sleep with a cooperative stomach, so work on this piece of the pie by experimenting with your eating and monitoring its effects on your ability to fall asleep.

Caffeine, alcohol, and heavy foods should be avoided right before you lay your pretty head down to rest. You don't need to be spinning in the bed.

It doesn't take much to curb a hunger pang before bedtime.

Drinking water keeps you feeling full and makes sure you don't go to bed dehydrated.

If your body tells you that's not enough, consider what these experts have to say.

Did your mama know what she was doing when she gave you cookies and milk before bed? Michael Breus, PhD. (called "The Sleep Doctor"), says you should not go to bed hungry and recommends a high-carbohydrate, low-protein snack sometime in the hour before bed.

Joy Bauer, the Resident Nutritionist of the Today's Show, says that although you should not eat a big meal too close to bedtime, you may want to choose a light carbohydrate snack that has tryptophan. Tryptophan helps you sleep better and elevates your mood. Everyone knows that turkey is a source of Tryptophan, but in reality it has no more than chicken or other meats and shellfish and because you may not want to have a lobster dinner right before bedtime consider some of the other sources of this amino acid: Beans, Whole Grains, Nuts and Seeds.

So what do I do? Sometimes with my cup of tea I mix in "Calm", a magnesium-calcium supplement that promotes relaxation. You can purchase Calm at any health food store or you can check this product out online at www.petergillham.com.

If I am really feeling hungry, I may choose a small piece of rice cake with a spread of peanut butter. I personally don't like the feeling of going to bed full, and I love waking in the morning feeling hungry for my breakfast. (I just hop right out of bed into my pumpkin pancakes, salivating at every thought of those yum-azing cakes). Breakfast is my favorite meal of the day, and so it increases my enjoyment to have an empty stomach ready to receive the amazing delish and nutrish gift of this meal. What is your thing?

If you are eating well throughout the day, you will sleep better at night. Specific foods high in tryptophan include broccoli, spinach, salmon, quinoa, lentils, and pinto beans. Shocking, right? All NAKED! See what I mean when I tell you that naked is the only way to eat? You get all you need from nakedness. Eat well, sleep well. Go figure! Since I mentioned figure...you should know by now your best figure will show up when you do all these things).

GET SOME BRIGHT EYE – THE RITUAL PART 2

Going to bed earlier and getting up earlier are two sides to the same coin. If you are going to stay up late and then try to wake up early, you will begrudge those early morning minutes rather than enjoy them. You have to start by shifting your current clock. Go to bed ten minutes earlier and wake up ten minutes earlier, and keep increasing by five-minute increments until you are in bed by your desired time. It's like weight training; you don't lift 15 pounds when you walk in the gym. You start with 5 and increase incrementally. This will prompt you to awaken earlier.

There are many benefits to rising early. As far back as our founding fathers, we've heard that "Early to bed, early to rise, makes a man healthy, wealthy and wise." You get quiet time with yourself when everyone else is still asleep. What can you do with an extra 10 minutes of morning? It's a great time to meditate or just sit and be with yourself. You can prepare a great healthy breakfast, or go for a walk or exercise. It gives you the opportunity to experience the sunrise. A whole universe of experience and quiet time activities are yours in those ten minutes. I personally love the morning, as it is my most productive time. In the warmer months, I go out for an early walk when there are no cars on the street, and the world is at peace with itself.

The best part of waking up is not the coffee in your house. If you're like me, it's the breakfast, so it would be just wrong of me to end my book without sharing my absolute favorite breakfast with you. Yes, I love oat jars and my shakes, but my pancakes are out of this world fabulous. Here is my amazing recipe for the best Naked pancakes that are so easy to make. They will help you lose weight, too. Pretty sure everyone will be excited to wake up to these babies.

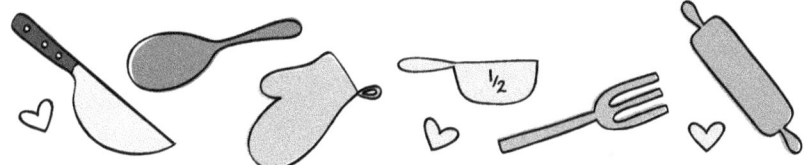

YUM. NAKED RECIPE:

NAKED POWER PUMPKIN PANCAKES

- 1/4 cup dry oats
- 4 egg whites
- 3 TBSP pure pumpkin (I use canned pumpkin or a leftover baked sweet potato)
- 1 tsp vanilla
- sprinkle of cinnamon and nutmeg

Mix in your blender and pour onto griddle. This recipe is one serving; it will make three small cakes or one giant cake, depending on your skillet and skill. This whole concoction is making just one serving, just for you. The good news is that you won't feel stuffed or tired after eating these, like you would if you were eating the "other" S.A.D. (Standard American Diet) pancake.

I spread the pancake with a dab of coconut creme (pure meat from the coconut—details are in your "Think Outside the Box Recommendations" at the back of the book). Drizzle with pure maple syrup and top with 1/2 cup warmed blueberries and 1TBSP chopped walnuts. Yum and double yum.

SMACK: (Get your head in the game)

Use your pretty head

I find that meditation, prayer, or even counting sheep like I did when I was a young girl, calms the mind and aids in falling asleep. Setting up a consistent nightly plan will help. I like to be in bed before 10 p.m. and unwind with a book, shut off the lights, and continue with a meditation or prayer. The ritual that gets you to sleep, keeps you asleep and helps you wake up rested and rejuvenated to participate fully in your day is the keeper, and it will be different for each of you.

I remember someone explained sleep to me by referencing an office building. She told me that when all the employees go home at night, the cleaning crew comes in to empty the garbage cans, wipe down the computers and phones, sweep the floor, straighten up, and generally freshen up the place so that the employees can come back the next day and get right down to business in a refreshed, clean environment. Your body is similar to that in many ways. During sleep our body restores and refreshes. Think about this analogy and you will understand why you need sleep, to make sure your brain and body space is cleaned and ready to rip roar the next day.

Dumping it all out, like the garbage can cleanup helps in the process of a restful sleep. Get a book and brain dump everything on your mind, including what you have to accomplish for the next day. Because we can't think two thoughts at the same time, this will set us up for sleep by pushing everything out of our heads for the evening.

A prayer of gratitude for the day can help you drift off to sleep in peace and contentment with thoughts of good things. Even after what may have felt like the worst day ever, you can find something worthy of thanks (even if the only thing you can think of today is the roof over your head and a nice warm bed to sleep in, that is good enough).

Your space must be sacred. Clear any clutter from your room and make it a retreat space. I have a very tiny bedroom, that I painted raspberry mousse, a beautiful dark pink color. How yummy delish it is having raspberry mousse walls staring back at you. It looks like a little jewelry box when I enter the room. I love it and it makes me happy to enter my room. I have favorite books, my lavender oil, a journal, and a pen by my bedside. It is my retreat and my sacred space.

Count your threads, not your calories.

Let's not forget the soft sheets. I would suggest that you purchase the most luxurious, high-thread count, quality, fabulous sheets you can afford so that you have luxury of their softness draping on and caressing your beautiful skin—because, of course, by now, you are sexy, hot, and confident enough to be sleeping naked!

Rosie's Rules for Sleeping Naked Like Baby After 40:

1. Take off your pjs before you get into bed feeling silky sheets next to your naked skin.

2. Strip down your worry and get rid of thoughts that are floating in your head. Release them to a journal or tomorrow's to do list.

3. Create your mini ritual list: Leave a notebook by your bed (to let go of worry), say a prayer (to let go of doubt), write down your gratitudes (to let go of resentment) and you'll sleep like a baby.

EXPERIENCE EXPERIMENT (Get your heart in the game)

Your Dream Book

Your vision may come in your sleep.

But you have the power to make your dreams real.

Part of the process of making your dreams a reality is to be aware of and acknowledge them. Here's the place and an opportunity to do that – Your very own, hand-crafted dream book.

This is not your ordinary arts-and-crafts project. It's an extraordinary manifestation of personal growth. It can change the direction of your life, spark your manifesting juices, and unlock your dreams, if you let it. Find a relaxing place. Light a beautiful candle.

It's time to dream big and commit your dreams to a dream book that will remind you of what it is you want and hope for your future. Create a beautiful atmosphere to work on your beautiful dreams. The candle is lit, some soft music is playing and you start to adorn your beautiful 8x10 notebook with colored pens, stickers ribbons, flowers, old but gorgeous magazines, anything beautiful to you. **These creative elements enable you to participate in your future by designing it today.**

Set a timer for at least thirty minutes and allow yourself the freedom to let creativity come in.

Take the magazines, scissors, markers, imagination, and timer. Shut off all phones, ringers, computers, blings, pings, and dings. Only love matters now, the love for yourself and the life you are creating for that special person that is you.

The main rule is to relax and let go. There is no wrong or right way. You are not going to mess up. Just let it flow. Don't worry if none of it makes sense or seems to go together. You can have random thoughts and pictures.

1. Cut out pictures from the magazines that appeal to you through color, vision, or feeling.

2. Cut out words with meaning; words that suggest what you like and want.

3. Make this YOUR book, full of your likes, inspirations, feelings, desires, wishes. Remember the collages you made back in grammar school? This is similar to that. It is a book about all that you love, desire, and dream up. If someone were to randomly pick up your book, it should feel and look like you, and they should be able to recognize that it is so you without seeing your name written on it. It's your essence, your values, your "style."

You'll be amazed at what shows up. You will notice how certain patterns and colors emerge as you just let go and play. You'll begin to see your favorite colors, houses, things to do, things to wear.

> "The key is to be real. Don't be afraid to put down what you really want. Express dreams big and small."

Don't let your "thinking thoughts" and "mind muddles" get in the way of what you put on that paper. Let it come from within you. Remember you can't mess this up—it's your book. It's your "naked" self coming through.

List 3 changes that you will implement in your life after reading this lesson:

1. _____
2. _____
3. _____

You've earned a rose.

The Big Bonus

The daily practice of small portions that will yield BIG results when practiced

BREATH

INTENTIONS

GRATITUDE

Time is critical for most of us, and most of us, most of the time, pop out of bed with a to-do list that, by its very nature, size and magnitude would not be possible to complete in one day.

We set ourselves up with a goal of getting everything done today; if not, we consider the day a complete or partial failure and beat ourselves up for not getting to it all. Then the overwhelmed feelings begin, and you know the drill. Not worth repeating here, but what is worth repeating is the system I have developed with small baby steps in a small amount of time that will yield big results if you are consistent with it.

Here's how it goes.

As soon as you awaken, lie in bed and give yourself ten more minutes. That's it! Just ten. Lie in the dark and start the BIG process.

Start with breath and focus only on breathing.
Breathe in to the count of five and out to the count of five.
Breathe in to the count of five and out to the count of five.
Breathe in to the count of five and out to the count of five.
Breathe in to the count of five and out to the count of five.
Breathe in to the count of five and out to the count of five.

Five times.

Only then turn your thoughts over and focus on your intentions for the day.

One sentence that you can remember, will help.

Maybe it is something like this:

"My intention for today is to really be relaxed when I sit and eat each meal."

or

"My intention for today is to call each one of my children and tell them I love them."

or

"My intention for today is to make sure I pet my pups for five minutes and love them up."

(Just one small thing that will make a big impact.)

Then focus on gratitude and appreciation.

Have a small pad by your bed so you can build this list. Jot down and repeat to yourself five things you are grateful for.

1. _____
2. _____
3. _____
4. _____
5. _____

You will be amazed at how much differently your day goes when you start it BIG (Breathing, Intention, Gratitude). (Don't forget that after you complete your ten-minute BIG, you'll need to eat a pure naked breakfast.) This is how each and every step in this book is connected; they all count, and they all matter; and when you put them all together, ultimately you find yourself in love—with yourself, your food, your body, and your life.

RESOURCE GUIDE
FOR BUILDING YOUR VERY OWN "THINK OUTSIDE THE BOX" SUPPORT BOX

This list of items are suggestions that can add support and enhance your experiences. You don't "have" to purchase them in order to participate fully but these are fun items, products and websites that will support your efforts and are lovely tools to use. For your convenience, I've listed my faves, my special things and their websites, so you can easily order them online. My Support Box is a combination of things to eat, think, wear, read, hear, experience and dream about.

- Very Dark Chocolate—this is a real superfood (not candy, but as delicious as candy can be)
- Vega Sport Performance Protein Products—If you gotta have a protein powder for those days you just can't get the food together, this is a totally yummy plant-based protein powder. Super nutrition and yummy delicious. (www.vegasport.com)
- Beautiful scented candles
- Relaxing meditation CD
- A hot new tube of lipstick—buy the newest, hottest, most daring color (check out the Chanel counter, the ultimate treat in luxurious lipsticks available at an upscale department store, and let them suggest a color to enhance your gorgeousness)
- Yummy teas (www.artoftea.com)
- New china cup (http://roses-and-teacups.com/teaware.php)
- New cake size and odd shaped plates (local thrift shops and garage sales are fun for this)
- Good sneakers/cross trainers/athletic shoes that are good to your feet—invest in your sneakers and show love to your feet
- Coconut cream—pure meat from the coconut (www.tropicaltraditions.com)
- Vitamix—amazing high-powered blender capable of changing your life (www.sleepingnakedafter40.com and click on the right side, on Vitamix)
- Rice cooker—makes perfect grains every time (Zojuruski Model No. NS-LAC05)
- A gorgeous notebook (available anywhere/even an old fashioned black and white marble notebooks works- add your favorite pix to the cover and make it your own gorgeous)
- Old magazines (sexy, sporty, eclectic, color ones)

- Rosie's Inspirational THE REAL DEAL deck of cards (email me at rosie@sleepingnakedafter40.com and I'll send you the link)
- The Naked Truth Journal—Your Journey in uncovering and discovering the real you with a guided journey loaded with fun and digging questions.
- Cooking Naked After 40—Create, Concoct & Cook
- Exercises and experiences in cooking skills and kitchen confidence with easy-to-follow recipes, using pure naked foods
- Other cooking and recipe books for learning yummy, delish, easy recipes. (Shop over at www.sleepingnakedafter40.com for a collection of recipes, products and books that support and encourage your new "naked" cooking and living)

Appreciate and acknowledge with gratitude every step along the way, and remember that you are exactly where you should be at all times!

Be proud that you have made this commitment to yourself, that you found the courage, determination and desire, that you are making changes every day and developing more and more confidence so that you can and will be sleeping naked!

As this book comes to a close, you need remember that:

YOU ARE AMAZING JUST THE WAY YOU ARE.

THANK YOU * THANK YOU * THANK YOU

I am beyond grateful for my one very precious life, and now that I am aware of how special it is, I appreciate it more and have made the choice to take extreme care of it in all the ways I shared with you.

Allowing me to share has deepened my passion for love as I realize the power in being in love with everything you do and participating fully in the process of self-love.

Thank you for being on the other end of this book and appreciating, accepting, and honoring how important you are in this world.

I hope that you have been inspired to love yourself, your body, your food, and your life, and to take extreme care of that gorgeous, healthy, sexy body, which is the temple of your soul. Do the best you can every day, in every way, at every workout, at every event, at every meal. Make every moment count, fall in love with that amazing gorgeous woman that is you.

With love and gratitude,

Ciao for now,

Rosie

More Naked Goodness

To help you on the path of sleeping naked, you may want to play harder and dig deeper as you discover "The Naked Truth". The Naked Truth guided journal is all about you and revealing the beauty that lies within. Asking poignant questions in fun creative ways, this book was designed to help you think outside the box and ask questions that you never have the time to think about. All you need is 15 minutes a day and a box of crayons to start the process of coloring your life with new feelings and thoughts of beauty, grace and love. Experience the art of moving forward with creativity and discovery by spending some quiet time with this book. Learn your ways to: Dine with Dignity, Age with Grace, Nourish with Love, and Participate in your Life with Joy, Abundance & Gratitude. It won't be long before you rediscover the magic of who you really are.

The new "real" healthy sexy you needs consistent nourishment and yum-azing naked food for your healthy, sexy body. The "Cooking Naked After 40" supplemental create, concoct and cook book is loaded with additional simple tips, ideas and recipes will further improve upon your cook naked skills.

Find the supplemental books on line at: www.sleepingnakedafter40.com/shop.

Other Naked Discoveries

For free recipes check out www.cookingnakedafter40.com

For food talk, self care tips, ideas and inspirations for women over 40, check out www.sleepingnakedafter40.com

For cooking video's, Sleeping Naked After 40 Lessons and how to's, check out www.youtube.com/rosiebattista

For Sleeping Naked After 40 Lessons in X-treme Self Love and X-traordinary Care, check out http://sleepingnakedafter40.com/promo/step-1.php

For irresistible, decadent, delicious healthy sweet treats you've got to have that you just can't make yourself and you just can't live without shop at: www.onesmartnakedcookie.com

For other books of this nature, shop at: www.sleepingnakedafter40.com/shop

Rosie Battista is Sleeping Naked After 40

Follow, Connect, Friend, Like and Watch here:

- www.twitter.com/rosiebattista
- www.linkin.com/in/rosiebattista
- www.facebook.com/rosiebattista/SNA40
- www.youtube.com/rosiebattista

About the Author:

Rosie is bold and bodacious. She is an inspirational teacher, preacher, and food "know-it-all", who really knows how to get you to lose the weight that has been hanging around annoyingly for years. She gets through to heart and head, and directs clients through implementable and sustainable step by step changes to life and style that are do-able and delicious.

Rosie is the author of multiple books: Sleeping Naked After 40, Cooking Naked After 40, and The Naked Truth, Sweetly Naked & Simply Naked. She's been featured in Oxygen Magazine and Get Off the Couch Special Edition and is a FabOverFifty contributor and nutrition/fitness guru. Her "Sleeping and Cooking Naked" programs were developed from personal experience and also extensive studies.

An EX- exclusive member of The 600 Pound Yo-Yo Weight Club, she lost the "diet mentality" and gained the experience necessary to help others in their food/weight/body image/mindset struggles. Rosie is an ACE Certified Personal Fitness Trainer and Weight Management Consultant, Figure Competitor and member of Organization of Competitor Body Builders, Graduate from Institute of Integrative Nutrition with Certification from Columbia University Teachers College, Integrative Nutrition Immersion Program, Certification from E-Cornell Plant Based Nutrition, NET Certified with Dr. Joel Fuhrman.

Rosie thrives in the NY Metro area with her two pugs, regular visits from her amazing kids and a big bunch of kale.

ABOUT THE COPY DOCTOR:

Alison Colby-Campbell of Alison's Brain4Rent stepped in on this second edition of Sleeping Naked After 40 as copy doctor, idea flesher-outer, and provided a second set of eyes and ears to ensure Rosie's voice stayed true to Rosie. And in the process, Alison absorbed Rosie's teachings to the point where she can step out of every pair of her old fatty jeans without stopping to unzip. Alison shops for local produce and is headquartered in the Greater Boston Area.

Other Naked Discoveries

For free recipes check out www.cookingnakedafter40.com

For food talk, self care tips, ideas and inspirations for women over 40, check out www.sleepingnakedafter40.com

For cooking video's, Sleeping Naked After 40 Lessons and how to's, check out www.youtube.com/rosiebattista

For Sleeping Naked After 40 Lessons in X-treme Self Love and X-traordinary Care, check out http://sleepingnakedafter40.com/promo/step-1.php

For irresistible, decadent, delicious healthy sweet treats you've got to have that you just can't make yourself and you just can't live without shop at: www.onesmartnakedcookie.com

For other books of this nature, shop at: www.sleepingnakedafter40.com/shop

Rosie Battista is Sleeping Naked After 40

Follow, Connect, Friend, Like and Watch here:

- www.twitter.com/rosiebattista
- www.linkin.com/in/rosiebattista
- www.facebook.com/rosiebattista/SNA40
- www.youtube.com/rosiebattista

About the Author:

Rosie is bold and bodacious. She is an inspirational teacher, preacher, and food "know-it-all", who really knows how to get you to lose the weight that has been hanging around annoyingly for years. She gets through to heart and head, and directs clients through implementable and sustainable step by step changes to life and style that are do-able and delicious.

Rosie is the author of multiple books: Sleeping Naked After 40, Cooking Naked After 40, and The Naked Truth, Sweetly Naked & Simply Naked. She's been featured in Oxygen Magazine and Get Off the Couch Special Edition and is a FabOverFifty contributor and nutrition/fitness guru. Her "Sleeping and Cooking Naked" programs were developed from personal experience and also extensive studies.

An EX- exclusive member of The 600 Pound Yo-Yo Weight Club, she lost the "diet mentality" and gained the experience necessary to help others in their food/weight/body image/mindset struggles. Rosie is an ACE Certified Personal Fitness Trainer and Weight Management Consultant, Figure Competitor and member of Organization of Competitor Body Builders, Graduate from Institute of Integrative Nutrition with Certification from Columbia University Teachers College, Integrative Nutrition Immersion Program, Certification from E-Cornell Plant Based Nutrition, NET Certified with Dr. Joel Fuhrman.

Rosie thrives in the NY Metro area with her two pugs, regular visits from her amazing kids and a big bunch of kale.

ABOUT THE COPY DOCTOR:

Alison Colby-Campbell of Alison's Brain4Rent stepped in on this second edition of Sleeping Naked After 40 as copy doctor, idea flesher-outer, and provided a second set of eyes and ears to ensure Rosie's voice stayed true to Rosie. And in the process, Alison absorbed Rosie's teachings to the point where she can step out of every pair of her old fatty jeans without stopping to unzip. Alison shops for local produce and is headquartered in the Greater Boston Area.

NAKED DISCLAIMER

ALL RIGHTS RESERVED

No part of this book may be reproduced or transmitted in any form whatsoever, electronic or mechanical, including photocopying, recording, or by any informational storage or retrieval system, without the express written, dated, and signed permission of the author.

DISCLAIMER AND/OR LEGAL NOTICES

The publication is for informational purposes only. While every attempt has been made to verify the information provided in this publication, neither the author nor her affiliates/partners assume any responsibility for errors, inaccuracies, or omissions. Any slights of people or organizations are unintentional. If advice concerning legal or related matters is needed, the services of a fully qualified professional should be sought.

All of the ideas and suggestions are opinions of the author. They are intended to provide information on health, wellbeing, and self-care. The author does not intend for her suggestions to take the place of medical advice or any other personal or professional services.

www.ingramcontent.com/pod-product-compliance
Lightning Source LLC
Chambersburg PA
CBHW080534170426
43195CB00016B/2559